Sleep Disorders

Psychological Disorders

Psychological Disorders

Sleep Disorders

Mary Brophy Marcus

Series Editor
Christine Collins, Ph.D.
Research Assistant Professor of Psychology
Vanderbilt University

Foreword by
Pat Levitt, Ph.D.
Director, Vanderbilt Kennedy Center
for Research on Human Development

CHELSEA HOUSE
PUBLISHERS
An imprint of Infobase Publishing

Sleep Disorders

Chelsea House
An imprint of Infobase Publishing
132 West 31st Street
New York NY 10001

Library of Congress Cataloging-in-Publication Data
Marcus, Mary Brophy.
    Sleep disorders / Mary Brophy Marcus.
        p. cm. — (Psychological disorders)
    Includes bibliographical references and index.
    ISBN-13: 978-1-60413-085-0 (alk. paper)
    ISBN-10: 1-60413-085-7 (alk. paper)
    1. Sleep disorders. I. Title.
    RC547.M37 2009
    616.8'498—dc22   2008035019

Chelsea House books are available at special discounts when purchased in
bulk quantities for businesses, associations, institutions, or sales promotions.
Please call our Special Sales Department in New York at (212) 967-8800 or
(800) 322-8755.

You can find Chelsea House on the World Wide Web at http://www.chelseahouse.com

Text design by Keith Trego
Cover design by Keith Trego and Ben Peterson

Printed in the United States of America

Bang EJB 10 9 8 7 6 5 4 3 2 1

This book is printed on acid-free paper.

All links and Web addresses were checked and verified to be correct at the time of
publication. Because of the dynamic nature of the Web, some addresses and links
may have changed since publication and may no longer be valid.

Table of Contents

Foreword

Pat Levitt, Ph.D.
Vanderbilt Kennedy
Center for Research
on Human Development

Think of the most complicated aspect of our universe, and then multiply that by infinity! Even the most enthusiastic of mathematicians and physicists acknowledge that the brain is by far the most challenging entity to understand. By design, the human brain is made up of billions of cells called neurons, which use chemical neurotransmitters to communicate with each other through connections called synapses. Each brain cell has about 2,000 synapses. Connections between neurons are not formed in a random fashion, but rather are organized into a type of architecture that is far more complex than any of today's supercomputers. And, not only is the brain's connective architecture more complex than any computer; its connections are capable of *changing* to improve the way a circuit functions. For example, the way we learn new information involves changes in circuits that actually improve performance. Yet some change can also result in a disruption of connections, like changes that occur in disorders such as drug addiction, depression, schizophrenia, and epilepsy, or even changes that can increase a person's risk of suicide.

Genes and the environment are powerful forces in building the brain during development and ensuring normal brain functioning, but they can also be the root causes of psychological and neurological disorders when things go awry. The way in which brain architecture is built before birth and in childhood will determine how well the brain functions when we are adults, and even how susceptible we are to such diseases as depression, anxiety, or attention disorders, which can severely disturb brain function. In a sense, then, understanding how the brain is built can lead us to a clearer picture of the ways in which our brain works, how we can improve its functioning, and what we can do to repair it when diseases strike.

Brain architecture reflects the highly specialized jobs that are performed by human beings, such as seeing, hearing, feeling, smelling, and moving. Different brain areas are specialized to control specific functions. Each specialized area must communicate well with other areas for the brain to accomplish even more complex tasks, like controlling body physiology—our patterns of sleep, for example, or even our eating habits, both of which can become disrupted if brain development or function is disturbed in some way. The brain controls our feelings, fears, and emotions; our ability to learn and store new information; and how well we recall old information. The brain does all this, and more, by building, during development, the circuits that control these functions, much like a hard-wired computer. Even small abnormalities that occur during early brain development through gene mutations, viral infection, or fetal exposure to alcohol can increase the risk of developing a wide range of psychological disorders later in life.

Those who study the relationship between brain architecture and function, and the diseases that affect this bond, are neuroscientists. Those who study and treat the disorders that are caused by changes in brain architecture and chemistry are psychiatrists and psychologists. Over the last 50 years, we have learned quite a lot about how brain architecture and chemistry work and how genetics contributes to brain structure and function. Genes are very important in controlling the initial phases of building the brain. In fact, almost every gene in the human genome is needed to build the brain. This process of brain development actually starts prior to birth, with almost all the neurons we will ever have in our brain produced by mid-gestation. The assembly of the architecture, in the form of intricate circuits, begins by this time, and by birth we have the basic organization laid out. But the work is not yet complete because billions of connections form over a remarkably long period of time, extending through puberty. The brain of a child is being built and modified on a daily basis, even during sleep.

While there are thousands of chemical building blocks, such as proteins, lipids, and carbohydrates, that are used much like bricks and mortar to put the architecture together, the highly detailed connectivity that emerges during childhood depends greatly upon experiences and our environment. In building a house, we use specific blueprints to assemble the basic structures, like a foundation, walls, floors, and ceilings. The brain is assembled similarly. Plumbing and electricity, like the basic circuitry of the brain, are put in place early in the building process. But for all of this early work, there is another very important phase of development, which is termed experience-dependent development. During the first three years of life, our brains actually form far more connections than we will ever need, almost 40 percent more! Why would this occur? Well, in fact, the early circuits form in this way so that we can use experience to mold our brain architecture to best suit the functions that we are likely to need for the rest of our lives.

Experience is not just important for the circuits that control our senses. A young child who experiences toxic stress, like physical abuse, will have his or her brain architecture changed in regions that will result in poorer control of emotions and feelings as an adult. Experience is powerful. When we repeatedly practice on the piano or shoot a basketball hundreds of times daily, we are using experience to model our brain connections to function at their finest. Some will achieve better results than others, perhaps because the initial phases of circuit-building provided a better base, just like the architecture of houses may differ in terms of their functionality. We are working to understand the brain structure and function that result from the powerful combination of genes building the initial architecture and a child's experience adding the all-important detailed touches. We also know that, like an old home, the architecture can break down. The aging process can be particularly hard on the ability of brain circuits to function at their best because positive change comes less readily as we get older. Synapses may be lost and brain chemistry can change over time. The difficulties in understanding how architecture gets built are paralleled by the complexities of what happens to that architecture as we grow older. Dementia associated with brain deterioration as a complication of Alzheimer's disease and memory loss associated with aging or alcoholism are active avenues of research in the neuroscience community.

There is truth, both for development and in aging, in the old adage "use it or lose it." Neuroscientists are pursuing the idea that brain architecture and chemistry can be modified well beyond childhood. If we understand the mechanisms that make it easy for a young, healthy brain to learn or repair itself following an accident, perhaps we can use those same tools to optimize the functioning of aging brains. We already know many ways in which we can improve the functioning of the aging or injured brain. For example, for an individual who has suffered a stroke that has caused structural damage to brain architecture, physical exercise can be quite powerful in helping to reorganize circuits so that they function better, even in an elderly individual. And you know that when you exercise and sleep regularly, you just feel better. Your brain chemistry and architecture are functioning at their best. Another example of ways we can improve nervous system function are the drugs that are used to treat mental illnesses. These drugs are designed to change brain chemistry so that the neurotransmitters used for communication between brain cells can function more normally. These same types of drugs, however, when taken in excess or abused, can actually damage brain chemistry and change brain architecture so that it functions more poorly.

As you read the Psychological Disorders series, the images of altered brain organization and chemistry will come to mind in thinking about complex diseases such as schizophrenia or drug addiction. There is nothing more fascinating and important to understand for the well-being of humans. But also keep in mind that as neuroscientists, we are on a mission to comprehend human nature, the way we perceive the world, how we recognize color, why we smile when thinking about the Thanksgiving turkey, the emotion of experiencing our first kiss, or how we can remember the winner of the 1953 World Series. If you are interested in people, and the world in which we live, you are a neuroscientist, too.

Pat Levitt, Ph.D.
Director, Vanderbilt Kennedy Center
for Research on Human Development
Vanderbilt University
Nashville, Tennessee

What Is Sleep?

Shortly after midnight on March 24, 1989, a 30,000-ton oil tanker called Exxon Valdez ran into a reef in Prince William Sound, Alaska. It spilled an estimated 11 million gallons of crude oil into the water—the largest oil spill in American history. The accident caused untold environmental damage, cost thousands of fishermen their livelihoods, and led to billions of dollars in cleanup costs. Fatigue was later cited as one of the reasons the ship's captain turned over the vessel's operation to a less-experienced crewmember that night, resulting in the tragic event.

Sleep. It's as important as food and water. Memory, performance, mood, and physical health all suffer when we're sleep-deprived. Research shows that with less than the recommended eight hours per night, we're more likely to get sick or die sooner than our well-rested counterparts. Other studies suggest that if we went too long without it, we'd die.[1] Sadly, some well-known human catastrophes have been linked to worker fatigue, including the Exxon Valdez oil spill and the explosion of the space shuttle Challenger.[2]

It makes sense that sleep plays such an important role in our lives considering humans spend one-third of their existence at rest—more time than most of us spend doing any other single activity. But what is actually happening to the body physically when we are slumbering? Scientists have differing opinions, yet all agree that the mystery of sleep is a complicated one to unravel. "We've learned that we do not sleep simply in order to get rid of sleepiness. Sleep performs essential biological functions. Those functions have not yet been fully established," says Michael Twery, Ph.D., the director of the National Center on Sleep Disorders Research Branch at the National Heart, Lung and Blood Institute, part of the National Institutes of Health.[3]

It is believed that the need for sleep is related to the amount of a chemical in the body known as **adenosine**. The longer a person stays awake, the higher the blood levels of this sleep-inducing compound become, resulting in a growing urge to nod off. On the other hand, as we sleep, levels of adenosine decrease. Substances such as **caffeine** and some drugs are considered stimulants because they help keep us perky when we're tired. On a physiological level, caffeine blocks the adenosine receptor, disrupting the chemical that sends the body drowsy cues.

Over the past several decades, scientists have gained a better understanding of the nature of sleep with the help of advances in biochemistry and technology. It has become easier for researchers to understand the chemical processes and genetic roots of **sleep disorders**. New and improved sleep-monitoring devices can track brain waves better. During sleep, an **electroencephalograph** can record brain wave activity, tracking the stages of normal sleep and helping to diagnose abnormalities in a person's sleep pattern. The result of an electroencephalograph test is an **electroencephalogram**, or EEG.

One of the challenges of better understanding sleep and correctly diagnosing patients with sleep disorders is that sleep problems occur when the patient is unconscious. This conundrum has spurred the growth of sleep centers around the country in the past several decades. There are now approximately 1,500 accredited sleep centers in the United States, according to the American Academy of Sleep Medicine. Sleep centers employ scientists and doctors who specialize in treating patients with sleep problems. At a sleep center, these specialists can monitor a person's nightly habits, such as twitching limbs and breathing disruptions.

A **polysomnogram (PSG)**, a sleep-recording device, may be used to measure brain activity, eye movements, muscle activity, heart rate and rhythm, blood pressure, and how much air the lungs are inhaling and exhaling. This test can also track the level of oxygen in a person's blood. A PSG is a painless procedure that involves placing numerous electrodes on the head that relay a patient's information to a computer.

Thanks to the PSG test and other forms of monitoring equipment, medical experts have discovered that the brain is actually quite busy when the sun goes down and slumber commences. During sleep, the human brain moves through distinct cycles in predictable patterns. Scientists who study sleep have linked each sleep stage to distinct electrical patterns in the brain, called brain waves. "Sleep is not just a single state. It is a very complex state. There are patterns. It is cyclical, but those cycles are changeable," says Twery.

When scientists monitor a patient's sleep, they are able to pinpoint patients who suffer from sleep disorders such as **insomnia**, **restless legs syndrome**, **narcolepsy**, and **sleep apnea**, among other conditions.

GOOD SLEEP

Before delving into the problems that can interfere with a healthy night's rest, it's important to understand normal sleep patterns. Everyone experiences a daily sleep-wake cycle, which includes about eight hours of nocturnal sleep and 16 hours of daytime wakefulness. This cycle is influenced by our **circadian rhythms**, or "biological clock." Circadian rhythms are the cyclical fluctuations in body temperature, hormone levels, and sleep that occur in any 24-hour period. All organisms have this fundamental clock, which is impacted by changes in the external environment, such as light and dark. The biological clock exists even in plants and bacteria—a universality that sleep experts say is not fully appreciated.

The human biological clock is actually a tiny bundle of cells called the suprachiasmatic nucleus (SCN), located in the area of the brain known as the **hypothalamus,** which releases the hormones that control sleep, body temperature, hunger, thirst, moods, and sex drive. The SCN responds to light signals received through the retina of the eye. External signals of light and darkness set the biological clock that determines when we're sleepy and when we're alert.[4]

When the sun goes down, the biological clock triggers the production of the hormone **melatonin**, which makes a person feel tired. Melatonin is produced by the **pineal gland**, which sits deep in the brain. Throughout the night, melatonin levels continue to increase, causing the drowsiest period for most people to fall between midnight and 7 a.m. There is typically a period of sleepiness midafternoon as well. The most wakeful period is during daylight hours, when melatonin levels are at their lowest.

When a person does not follow the natural circadian rhythms that regulate sleeping and waking—perhaps because they work a night shift—or when the seasons change and light and temperature fluctuate, the circadian clock has to adjust to the change. If it does not realign easily, problems such as jet lag and some types of sleep disorders can occur.

Before the light bulb was invented, most folks went to bed shortly after sunset, especially people tied to farming lifestyles. In our 24/7 society, however, many individuals have trouble abiding by their biological clocks. The Centers for Disease

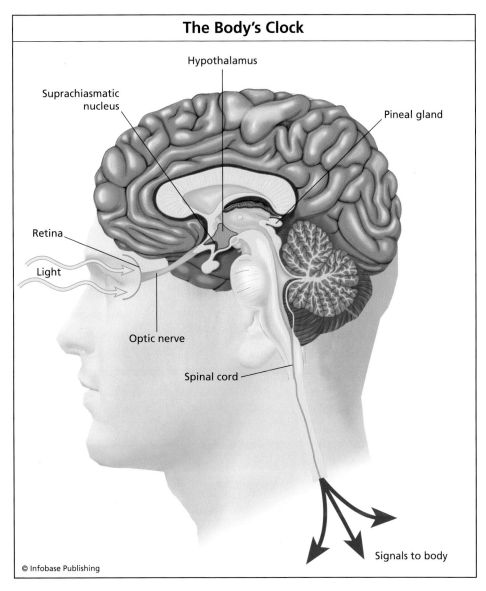

The Body's Clock

Hypothalamus

Suprachiasmatic
nucleus

Pineal gland

Retina

Light

Optic nerve

Spinal cord

Signals to body

© Infobase Publishing

Figure 1.1 The human biological clock is actually a tiny bundle of cells called the suprachiasmatic nucleus (SCN), located in the part of the brain known as the hypothalamus, which releases the hormones that control sleep and other bodily functions. The SCN responds to light signals received through the retina of the eye. External signals of light and darkness set the biological clock that determines when we're sleepy and when we're alert. The SCN then signals the pineal gland to release the hormone melatonin, which makes the body feel tired.

Control and Prevention estimates that between 30 percent and 40 percent of American adults do not obtain adequate sleep within a yearlong period. Perhaps it is because nearly 25 percent of Americans work night or evening shifts. More than two-thirds of night-shift workers have sleep problems.[5] Overly tired workers employed at the Three Mile Island nuclear power plant near Middletown, Pennsylvania, who made mistakes on

Sleep Myths

Myth: Napping is only for children.

Fact: Infants, toddlers, the sick, and the elderly are not the only ones who can benefit from an afternoon nap. Somehow, over the years, Americans have associated healthy adults who nap with being lazy, but a daytime nap can help make you more alert, quicker on your feet, and a clearer thinker, according to some sleep researchers. Famous siesta-takers include Winston Churchill and President Lyndon Johnson.

Myth: Sleep is a time when your body and brain shut down.

Fact: There is no scientific evidence that indicates that the body's major organs shut down, including the brain. Researchers have discovered that some physiological processes work harder. For instance, the secretion of some hormones increases and certain parts of the brain show more activity.

Myth: Extra sleep at night can cure excessive daytime fatigue.

Fact: Quantity of sleep is key to a healthier, happier you, but quality of sleep is equally important. Adults with a sleep disorder, such as sleep apnea, may get more than the recommended eight to nine hours a night but often still feel unrested in the morning. This is because their disorder is the job, were believed to have played a role in the equipment malfunctions that led to a partial meltdown that occurred there on March 28, 1979.[6]

STAGES OF SLEEP

There are two basic types of sleep: **REM sleep** (rapid eye movement sleep) and **non-REM (NREM)** sleep.

---

interrupting the normal sleep cycles. Treatment of these sleeping disorders can help, though.

Myth: One hour less of sleep a night won't make a big difference the next day.

Fact: Recent research shows that even one less hour a night can reduce your ability to think clearly and respond quickly. It can compromise your body's ability to beat infection, your heart health, and energy level. If you regularly miss out on sleep, you'll tally a sleep debt that will leave you extremely tired by day.[7]

Myth: Putting a baby to bed later will mean she'll sleep later in the morning.

Fact: Weary parents are doing some wishful thinking if they think keeping their little one up later will avoid those 6 a.m. wake-up cries and buy them some extra hours of sleep the next morning. Babies sleep better, longer, and cry less if they are put to bed early in the evening. Babies who go to sleep late in the evening are often overtired. Babies may show "sleep signals"—eye rubbing, yawning, and slowing down—as early as 6 or 7 p.m., and parents need to heed their needs and settle them down for the night.

Non-REM Sleep

In most adults, sleep begins with non-REM sleep. According to the American Academy of Sleep Medicine, non-REM sleep encompasses about 75 percent to 80 percent of an adult's total

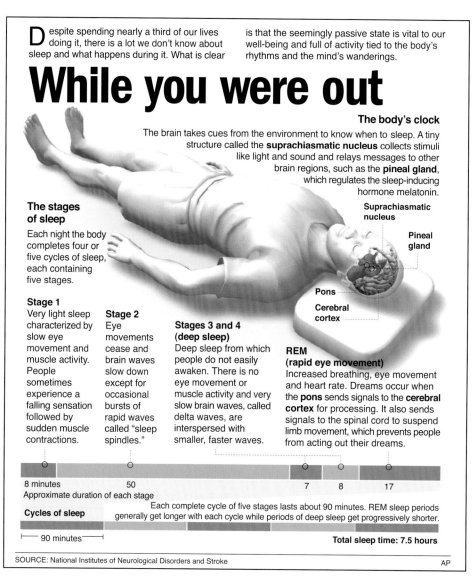

Despite spending nearly a third of our lives doing it, there is a lot we don't know about sleep and what happens during it. What is clear is that the seemingly passive state is vital to our well-being and full of activity tied to the body's rhythms and the mind's wanderings.

While you were out

The body's clock

The brain takes cues from the environment to know when to sleep. A tiny structure called the **suprachiasmatic nucleus** collects stimuli like light and sound and relays messages to other brain regions, such as the **pineal gland**, which regulates the sleep-inducing hormone melatonin.

Suprachiasmatic nucleus

Pineal gland

Pons

Cerebral cortex

The stages of sleep

Each night the body completes four or five cycles of sleep, each containing five stages.

Stage 1
Very light sleep characterized by slow eye movement and muscle activity. People sometimes experience a falling sensation followed by sudden muscle contractions.

Stage 2
Eye movements cease and brain waves slow down except for occasional bursts of rapid waves called "sleep spindles."

Stages 3 and 4 (deep sleep)
Deep sleep from which people do not easily awaken. There is no eye movement or muscle activity and very slow brain waves, called delta waves, are interspersed with smaller, faster waves.

REM (rapid eye movement)
Increased breathing, eye movement and heart rate. Dreams occur when the **pons** sends signals to the **cerebral cortex** for processing. It also sends signals to the spinal cord to suspend limb movement, which prevents people from acting out their dreams.

8 minutes   50   7   8   17
Approximate duration of each stage

Cycles of sleep
Each complete cycle of five stages lasts about 90 minutes. REM sleep periods generally get longer with each cycle while periods of deep sleep get progressively shorter.

90 minutes

Total sleep time: 7.5 hours

SOURCE: National Institutes of Neurological Disorders and Stroke   AP

Figure 1.2 © *AP Images*

sleep time and comprises four stages. Stage 1 non-REM sleep is light and a person is easy to wake up at this time. Nearby noise may also disturb a person at this stage of sleep back into wakefulness. During this light sleep, brain waves and eye activity slow down. A stage 1 sleeper may experience the sensation of falling, ending in a sudden muscle jerk.

In stage 2 non-REM sleep, also considered a light sleep period, eye movement stops. Patients whose brain waves are monitored in a **sleep lab** will show a distinctive pattern of slower brain waves, interrupted with occasional bursts of rapid waves, called sleep spindles. The heart rate drops, as does body temperature.

As one's body moves into stage 3 non-REM sleep, brain waves slow down even more, though there are periods of smaller, faster waves at times. In stage 4 non-REM sleep, brain waves are very slow most of the time. There is no eye movement and very little muscle activity. Stages 3 and 4 of non-REM sleep are called slow-wave sleep and are considered the deep sleep phases. Slow or delta waves are present on **EEGs** at this time. Blood pressure drops, body temperature falls even lower, and breathing slows as the body becomes almost motionless.

If you tried to wake up a friend or family member during slow-wave sleep, it would be difficult to rouse them. They would probably feel groggy and need a few minutes to become oriented. This phase of rest is often referred to as the "restorative" part of sleep. Sleep experts believe you need stages 3 and 4 of non-REM sleep in order to feel awake and energetic the next day. Stages 3 and 4 are also stages during which certain sleep problems tend to occur. For example, some children experience bed-wetting, **night terrors**, or sleepwalking during stages 3 and 4 of non-REM sleep.

REM Sleep

Rapid eye movement sleep is the most active period of sleep, when intense brain activity occurs. Brain waves are quick, a lot like those observed during the waking state. Breathing is more rapid and irregular, and the eyes (usually still closed) move quickly in numerous directions. Limb muscles become temporarily paralyzed—a state called *atonia.* Eye muscles and muscles related to respiration and cardiovascular activity become more active. Heart rate and blood pressure increase. REM sleep is often called dream sleep, and it's believed that this is the period of sleep when most dreams occur. While most people remain fairly immobile during REM sleep, except for occasional muscle twitching, there is an exception. In those with **REM sleep behavior disorder,** discussed in more detail in Chapter 5, the individual does not have typical REM-related muscle paralysis. He or she may actually act out their dream—gesticulating, punching, even running—which can be dangerous to the sleeper and his or her cohabitants.

Sleep experts increasingly believe that REM sleep also plays a key role in maintaining a healthy body. Many recent studies examining the effects of sleep deprivation on humans support the idea. What's more, animal studies suggest the same. Rats typically live for two to three years, but they survive only about five weeks when deprived of REM sleep. When deprived of all sleep, they live only two to three weeks, a time period similar to death because of lack of food and water.[8]

BALANCED SLEEP

Doctors have not defined with certainty the role each stage of sleep plays in terms of mental and physical health, but they do know that obtaining the right balance is key and allows for restful sleep and healthy functioning during waking hours.

The sleep cycle

The two types of sleep (NREM and REM) alternate in cycles of roughly 90 minutes throughout the sleep period. The length of REM sleep periods increases as the cycle progresses. Most people experience four or five cycles per night.

EEGs Electroencephalograms (EEGs) are recordings of the brain's electrical activity – "brain waves." EEGs can be used to monitor the brain's electrical activity during sleep. Different types of waves are associated with the different stages of the sleep cycle.

1 Awake
When a person is awake, EEGs typically record beta waves, which are associated with arousal, alertness, and mental activity.

2 NREM sleep: stage one
The eyes are closed and relaxation begins; body temperature, respiration, pulse, and blood pressure are normal. The EEG shows alpha waves.

3 NREM sleep: stage two
The eyes roll from side to side; the EEG pattern becomes irregular.

4 NREM sleep: stage three
Sleep deepens, and the EEG shows theta and delta waves. Body temperature, respiration, pulse, and blood pressure decline; skeletal muscles become very relaxed.

5 NREM sleep: stage four
The EEG shows delta waves. Body temperature, respiration, pulse, and blood pressure are at their lowest levels; skeletal muscles are very relaxed. Bedwetting or sleepwalking may occur in stage four.

6 REM sleep
The cycle then reverses through stage four, three, and two, but instead of waking into stage one, the sleeper enters REM sleep. The EEG shows similar patterns as for the awake state. It is in REM sleep that most dreams occur.

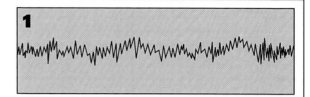

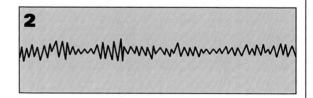

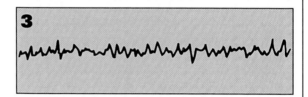

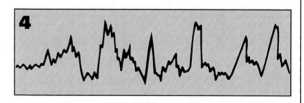

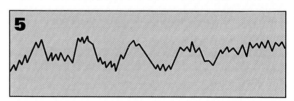

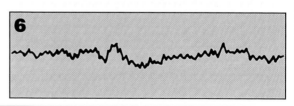

Figure 1.3 © *Diagram Visual Information/Human Physiology On File*

Research indicates that the amount of sleep that is ideal for an individual is related to their age. Adults need anywhere from seven to nine hours of sleep every night, while teenagers benefit from about 9.5 hours. Infants thrive on about 16-18 hours of sleep per day. Quality of rest, however, is as pivotal as quantity. The right mix of REM and non-REM sleep—a predictable pattern called *sleep architecture*—throughout the night determines whether someone feels well-rested.

A complete **sleep cycle** consists of NREM and REM cycles that alternate every 90 to 110 minutes and is repeated four to six times per night, though this pattern may vary among various adult age groups. Adults spend more than half of their total daily sleep time in stage 2 sleep, and the remaining time in the other stages, but the amount of time spent in any given state is not constant over the course of a night.

The first sleep cycles each night include short periods of REM sleep and longer periods of slow-wave sleep. As the night progresses, REM episodes increase in length and slow-wave sleep decreases. By morning, all sleep is in stages 1, 2, and REM.

Sleep architecture also varies over the course of a lifetime. Normal adults spend up to 25 percent of sleep time in REM, but new babies spend almost half of their resting hours in REM sleep. Young children also have significant amounts of deep NREM sleep, but as people age, stages 3 and 4 NREM slow-wave sleep decrease, with lighter sleep predominating. Sleep quality changes with age, but the need for sleep does not decrease, as is often believed.[9]

Why We Need Sleep

Patty, a 38-year-old mother of three who teaches Latin in high *school, admits she burns the candle at both ends. She counts herself lucky if she can get at most five or six hours of sleep each night. It's not uncommon for her to fall asleep in the evening before she has even changed into her pajamas and crawled into bed, says her husband, Jim, who often wakes her when she's dozed off on the family couch. She can't seem to fit more rest into her schedule, and admits that sleep is just not a priority. "I have things to do and not enough hours in the day," she says.*

Patty admits that she is often sleepy and relies on lattes and cola to keep her energized, and though she hasn't experienced any serious fatigue-related problems, little signs indicate she needs to get more sleep at night. Not long ago, she was correcting a batch of papers late at night and fell asleep sitting up. When she awoke she found a large ink stain had soaked through the entire stack of her students' papers. "I was so tired I fell asleep in the middle of grading. When they saw the papers, I think my students could guess exactly what had happened," she says, admitting it was not the first time that such an incident had occurred.

Patty is one of millions of Americans who regularly gets less than the recommended amount of sleep that doctors say humans need to ward of illness and function well each day. According to the Sleep Foundation's 2002 Sleep in America poll, Americans average 6.9 hours of sleep on weeknights and 7.5 hours per night on weekends. That's a far cry from the days before Thomas Edison's light bulb became a common household fixture. In 1910, for example, most people slept nine hours a night.[10] According to the Sleep Foundation poll, 47 million Americans do not meet their daily minimum for sleep, which puts them at risk for accidents and injury. What's more, millions of cases of sleep disorders are going undiagnosed because Americans do not consider sleepiness a health risk, according to National Commission on Sleep Disorders research.

WHY SLEEP?

"When there is so much to do in each day, why bother wasting hours in bed?" ask busy Americans. Theories about why we need to get off our feet and rest our bodies for a portion of every 24-hour period vary among experts, but when scientists look across the animal kingdom—from bugs to bats to whales—it is clear that sleep is necessary for survival of all creatures. How much each species needs varies, perhaps because of an animal's status as prey or predator, or maybe sleep needs are related to an organism's size or metabolism. These are questions researchers are still trying to answer in humans, and in other species.

"In general, we don't understand why we need sleep. But what we're learning is that what happens in the third of our lives when we're asleep is just as important as what happens when we are awake, even though it's still much less understood," says Richard Castriotta of Memorial Hermann Hospital Sleep Disorders Center in Houston.[11] The daily drive for sleep may be due in part to a natural chemical in the body known as adenosine, which builds up in the brain while awake. During sleep, adenosine is broken down by the body. The more adenosine builds up in the body, the greater one's **sleep debt**.

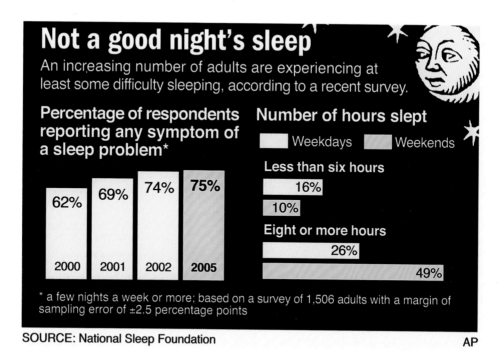

Not a good night's sleep

An increasing number of adults are experiencing at least some difficulty sleeping, according to a recent survey.

Percentage of respondents reporting any symptom of a sleep problem*

62%	69%	74%	75%
2000	2001	2002	2005

Number of hours slept

☐ Weekdays   ☐ Weekends

Less than six hours
16%
10%

Eight or more hours
26%
49%

* a few nights a week or more; based on a survey of 1,506 adults with a margin of sampling error of ±2.5 percentage points

SOURCE: National Sleep Foundation   AP

Figure 2.1 © *AP Images*

Recent research indicates that getting enough rest helps people ward off illness, recover from injury, stay alert, retain new information, and generally have a better outlook on life. According to National Institutes of Health reports, lack of sleep can also inhibit the body's ability to produce insulin and boost one's risk of diabetes. Other research shows that people who sleep the least are more apt to be diagnosed with high blood pressure, depression, and heart disease.[12]

Researchers have learned that during sleep, many of the body's major organ and regulatory systems continue to work actively, including certain parts of the brain that actually increase their activity dramatically. The body produces more of certain hormones as well.

DAILY NEEDS

How much sleep you need to stay well is still being debated, and different experts and groups may prescribe slightly varied amounts. In one study that tracked a million adults ages 30 to 102 and that was conducted by researchers at the University of California, San Diego, and the American Cancer Society, there was a higher mortality rate among those who slept less than four hours as well as in those who slept more than eight hours a night. Sleepers who clocked an average of six to seven hours of sleep each night experienced the lowest death rates.[13] Currently, national sleep recommendations advise adults to obtain eight hours of sleep a night, but most sleep experts say that's an average and sleep needs actually vary from person to person. More research is needed to determine whether the national figure should remain the same.[14]

Day to day, experts have found that sleep requirements remain consistent. Sleep specialists say they are just now beginning to understand how much sleep humans need at different times in their lives in order to feel good and function healthfully.

Sleep needs seem to vary across our lives, beginning with highest sleep requirements in infancy, then tapering down during mid-childhood and the teen years, and remaining steady through the adult and older-adult years. Newborns should sleep 16 to 18 hours a day; preschool children, 10 to 12 hours; school-age children and adolescents, at least 9 hours; and adults, 8 to 8.5 hours, although individual needs may vary by an hour either up or down.

If you do not get the rest you need at night—even one hour less—a sleep debt can develop, although napping or extra sleep on subsequent nights can help reduce it or keep it at bay. Without enough sleep, mental and physical functioning may be impaired. Studies show that the more sleep debt you tally, the

Figure 2.2 Sleep needs vary across life, beginning with the highest sleep requirements in infancy. © *Jason Lugo/iStockphoto Inc.*

worse you function. Even if you do not feel sleepy when you're in sleep debt, your daily performance may go down and your risk for accidents and injury go up.

Growing children can be severely affected by sleep debt. Unfortunately, millions do not get the hours they need each day. In a 2006 report in the journal *Pediatrics*, Columbia University School of Nursing researchers reported that about 15 million American children are affected by inadequate sleep. A child who doesn't get an adequate night's sleep is at high risk for symptoms of physical and mental impairment. He or she may fall asleep in school, have difficulty concentrating, and exhibit behavioral problems.

Instead of acting lethargic, as one might expect a sleep-deprived child to behave, it's not uncommon for youngsters

Table 2.1 Brown bats need 19 hours of sleep a day, while giraffes need less than two. Humans fall somewhere in the middle.

AVERAGE SLEEP NEEDS		
SPECIES	AVERAGE TOTAL SLEEP TIME (% OF 24 HR)	AVERAGE TOTAL SLEEP TIME (HOURS/DAY)
Brown Bat	82.9%	19.9 hr
Python	75.0%	18.0 hr
Owl Monkey	70.8%	17.0 hr
Human (infant)	66.7%	16.0 hr
Tiger	65.8%	15.8 hr
Squirrel	62.0%	14.9 hr
Lion	56.3%	13.5 hr
Cat	50.6%	12.1 hr
Rabbit	47.5%	11.4 hr
Dog	44.3%	10.6 hr
Baboon	42.9%	10.3 hr
Chimpanzee	40.4%	9.7 hr
Guinea Pig	39.2%	9.4 hr
Human (adult)	33.3%	8.0 hr
Pig	32.6%	7.8 hr
Guppy (fish)	29.1%	7.0 hr
Gray Seal	25.8%	6.2 hr
Human (elderly)	22.9%	5.5 hr
Cow	16.4%	3.9 hr
African Elephant	13.8%	3.3 hr
Horse	12.0%	2.9 hr
Giraffe	7.9%	1.9 hr

Source: Used with the permission of Dr. Eric H. Chudler, Neuroscience for Kids, University of Washington, http://faculty.washington.edu/chudler/neurok.html

who are chronically tired to act agitated, inattentive, irritable, easily frustrated, or to have trouble modulating their impulses. They may be misdiagnosed as hyperactive or with behavioral problems, and then incorrectly medicated. "Adequate nighttime sleep is just as important as healthy eating and exercise for children's development," says Claude Lenfant, M.D., former director of the National Heart, Lung, and Blood Institute.[15]

EFFECTS OF SLEEP DEPRIVATION

Many American adults today are lucky if they tally the recommended eight hours of sleep a night. Chronic fatigue from lack of sleep is a pandemic, according to physician and sleep research pioneer William C. Dement of Stanford University. As many as 15 percent of Americans are sleep deprived, according to experts at the National Institutes of Health. A host of factors play a role, including the combined responsibilities of work, child care, and household requirements. Societal pressures to work longer hours, and on weekends, and to pull more night shifts have caused Americans to reduce their sleep time by about 20 percent over the past century. Over the past three decades, Americans have added an additional 158 hours—almost one full month—to their work schedules annually.[16] Ongoing financial worries, relationship issues, chronic illness, and layoffs are among the personal issues that keep people tossing and turning at night.

Sleep deprivation can have devastating effects on the body's functioning. In an animal study, rats that were denied sleep over several weeks died, leading scientists to deduce that sleep is as necessary to thriving as food and water. According to the National Institutes of Health, when rats were denied REM sleep, they lived only five weeks, when the normal lifespan of a rat is two to three years. Deprived of all sleep, the rats survived only two to three weeks, the same timeframe it takes for them to die of starvation.[17]

SLEEP AND MENTAL FUNCTIONING

In the past few decades, a plethora of research and statistics have shown that sleep deprivation negatively impacts memory, mood, creativity, acuity, and productivity—even personal relationships. A 2007 National Sleep Foundation poll showed that romance takes a plunge when people aren't getting adequate rest. Another study by scientists at the University of Pennsylvania in 2003 found that cognitive performance decreased when subjects obtained less than eight hours of sleep at night.[18]

Evidence of this decrease in functioning includes the case of one sleep-deprived mother from Wisconsin, whose 6-month-old died after she left it in the car for more than eight hours after she forgot to drop the child at daycare before going to work. The mother was not charged with neglect or abuse; reports indicated that it was an accident due to sleep deprivation.[19]

On the flip side, a little extra sleep in the form of a nap may boost mental capacity. Results from a study by Weill Cornell Medical College researchers suggest that older people get a mental boost from short naps, casually called "catnaps" or "power naps." A January 2005 study published in the *Journal of the American Geriatrics Society* followed 32 healthy people, ages 55–85, for two three-night, three-day sessions. Study subjects took naps on some days and on other days were instructed to go without a nap. On nap days, they were allowed to sleep for two hours during the day. Some nappers slept as briefly as 12 minutes, while others took advantage of almost all of the two-hour naptime they were allotted. On non-nap days, study subjects could rest but weren't allowed to sleep during the day.

Though it took them slightly longer to fall asleep at night on napping days, the nappers tallied more total sleep minutes on their nap days, and on the following day, they scored better on tests that tracked reasoning, reaction time, and perception.[20]

SLEEP AND THE IMMUNE SYSTEM

While scientists don't yet fully understand physiologically how a deficit of sleep affects disease, research shows links between sleep and the body's immune system. When University of Chicago sleep scientist Eve van Cauter exposed sleep-deprived students—allowed four hours of sleep a night for six nights—to flu vaccine, she reported that their immune systems produced only half the normal number of antibodies in response to the virus. She also found that the subjects became somewhat insulin resistant, which has been linked with weight gain and diabetes. Cortisol, a hormone associated with stress, increased, and the students' heart rates and blood pressure went up as well.[21]

Physiologic studies suggest that a sleep deficit may put the body into a state of high alert, in which stress hormones are produced faster, ratcheting up blood pressure. What's more, sleep-deprived humans have shown elevated levels of immunologic proteins in the blood called *cytokines,* which indicate a heightened state of inflammation in the body, according to a study published in the *Archives of Internal Medicine* by UCLA scientists in 2006. Study results showed an apparent link between sleep loss and inflammation—and inflammation is believed to contribute to a higher risk for certain diseases.[22]

When sleep is chronically truncated, health risks are magnified. Diabetes, obesity, cancer, and heart disease are all now linked to erratic and poor sleep habits.[23]

One large epidemiological study by Harvard Medical School scientists, involving 71,617 women nurses, found that in a 10-year period, 934 cases of coronary heart disease (CHD) were reported. Mortality rates were higher in nurses who reported sleeping fewer than six hours a night compared to those who slept more. In the study, sleeping five hours or less per night was associated with a 30 percent increase in risk of CHD, and

Drowsy Driving Costs Lives

Drowsy driving causes at least 100,000 police-reported crashes annually, resulting in more than 40,000 injuries and 1,550 deaths each year, according to the National Highway Traffic Safety Administration. In addition, drowsy-driving accidents are believed to be widely underreported due to a lack of uniformity in crash reporting across the United States. In an effort to combat drowsy driving and foster awareness of the issue, the National Sleep Foundation launched the Drowsy Driving Prevention Week in 2007. DrowsyDriving.org, a special Web site dedicated to the initiative, provides information on efforts nationwide by a variety of organizations to reduce drowsy driving.

Figure 2.3 Drowsy driving puts lives at risk. © *Carol and Mike Werner/Phototake*

sleeping six hours per night was associated with an 18 percent greater risk. Women who slept eight hours per night had the lowest recorded rate of CHD.[24]

According to the National Institute of Neurological Disorders and Stroke, the immune system is closely linked to **neurons** that control sleep. When humans get sick, we tend to feel sleepy. Scientists think this probably happens because when our immune system begins fighting off disease, we release chemicals called cytokines that cause sickness behaviors, such as drowsiness, malaise, and a drop in mood. By sleeping, it's thought that the body may be using more of its resources to heal.[25]

THE SLEEP–BLOOD PRESSURE CONNECTION

A report published in 2006 in the journal *Hypertension* suggested that long-term sleep deprivation increases the risk of high blood pressure, also called **hypertension**. The study, conducted by Columbia University physicians, examined the link between blood pressure and sleep was conducted in 4,810 participants between the ages of 32 and 86. Subjects between the ages of 32 and 59 who slept less than six hours a night had more than double the risk of high blood pressure than did those who slept more than six hours a night. Study results suggest that people who sleep for only short periods—less than six hours a night—increase their average blood pressure and heart rate. Over time, the researchers suggested, this could lead to persistent high blood pressure. It was concluded that increasing amount and quality of sleep may play a role in the treatment and prevention of high blood pressure in people younger than 60.[26]

Another study shows that napping can play a role in lowering blood pressure. *The Journal of Applied Physiology* published a small online study that tested nine healthy volunteers who did not typically nap. Each subject slept four hours the night before the test, then was hooked up to a device that checked blood

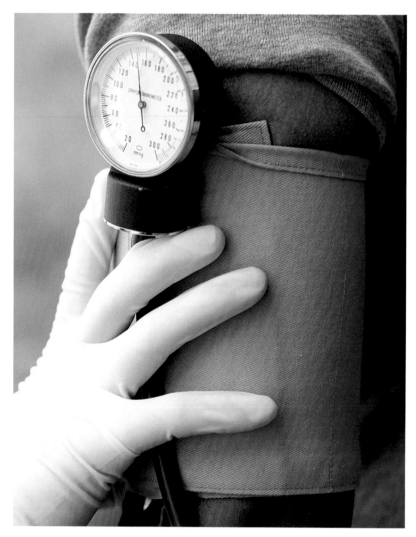

Figure 2.4 Studies link long-term sleep deprivation with increased risk of hypertension. © Sandeep Subba/iStockphoto Inc.

pressure under three different conditions: In two sessions the volunteers were allowed to relax, once when standing and once while lying down, but were not allowed to fall sleep. In the third session, the study subjects were given permission to fall asleep for no more than an hour.

Researchers conducting this study at John Moores University in Liverpool noted a significant drop in blood pressure in the napping group, but not in the groups that relaxed without being allowed to doze off. Also, researchers observed a significant drop in blood pressure in the napping group. The drop in blood pressure came just before falling asleep, not during the actual nap, leaving researchers to conclude that perhaps the anticipation of a nap, real sleep to come, was key to napping's benefits.[27]

SLEEP AND APPETITE

Studies in adults and children link less sleep with obesity, although why this happens is still being explored. Researchers do know that as we sleep, hormones are released that help modulate hunger cues and the body's use of energy. People who get fewer hours of sleep on a regular basis appear to have higher levels of the hormone **ghrelin**, which causes hunger, and low levels of **leptin**, a hormone related to calorie intake that normally helps curb appetite.[28]

In a study published in the December 2004 issue of *Annals of Internal Medicine*, University of Chicago scientists concluded that in healthy young men, short sleep duration was associated with decreased leptin levels, while ghrelin levels were increased, as were hunger and appetite.[29]

Sleep Tips

Sometimes varying your bedtime routine or changing a bad habit can have a positive influence on sleep. These behavior-modifying tips may contribute to better sleep.

Set regular sleep hours.

Go to bed and get up at the same time every day, even on weekends. Sticking to a schedule helps reinforce your body's sleep-wake cycle.

Minimize snacks before bedtime.

Too much food and liquid can cause heartburn or wake you up repeatedly in the night for bathroom trips.

Avoid nicotine, caffeine, and alcohol in the evening.

These stimulants can keep you awake. Avoid coffee, tea, and chocolate as many as eight hours before bedtime. Although alcohol is often believed to be a sedative, it actually disrupts sleep.

Exercise regularly but not too close to bedtime.

Regular physical activity, especially aerobic exercise, can help you fall asleep faster and make your sleep more restful—but don't work out too close to hitting the hay. Give your heart and muscles time to slow down.

Create a cool, dark, quiet bedroom.

Use blackout curtains, eye covers, earplugs, extra blankets, a white noise machine, a fan, a CD of peaceful sounds, a humidifier—whatever it takes to make your bedroom a peaceful, sleep-inducing sanctuary.

Develop a pre-bedtime routine and stick to it.

A warm bath, some light reading, or meditation prior to hopping under the covers each night prepares your body for a good night's rest.

Avoid upsetting activities right before sleep.

Save bill paying, housework, and computer activities for earlier in the day. They can over-stimulate and upset you, making sleep elusive.

Kick the television out of the bedroom.

Some research indicates that watching TV in bed, before going to sleep, stimulates the body, interfering with the ability to fall off within 10 to 15 minutes.

Don't nap past 3 p.m.

Naps can help you catch up from a sleep deficit, but snoozing too late in the afternoon can interfere with quality night sleep.

Figure 2.5 Avoid caffeine, alcohol, and nicotine in the evening for better sleep. © *Jozsef Szasz-Fabian/iStockphoto Inc.*

3 Insomnia

Alissa, a 23-year-old public relations associate from Philadelphia, says sleep has never come easily. "Even as a child, my mom says I always wanted to stay awake, be part of the action," Alissa explains. But now, with the stresses of a full-time job and adult life, sleep is even more elusive, she notes. Up until midnight or later most nights, Alissa finds herself still washing dishes, tidying the house, or watching television. Even though she is tired, she says, "I'll do anything instead of just lying in bed feeling anxious about not sleeping."

The repercussions of limited sleep are noticeable in her daily life. "I am cranky. I just want to get everything over with so that I can lay down. I am not unmotivated, but I am more easily annoyed. I complain more when I am tired," Alissa says. Often fatigued, she prefers not to drive on long trips, since the monotonous rhythm of the car and her tendency to be tired is a worrisome combination, and often she plans her days and weekends around naps. Prior to one recent wedding she was invited to, Alissa arranged to skip the ceremony because she knew from experience that she would be tired by that time in the afternoon. "I knew I would need a nap at that hour if I was going to stay up and enjoy the reception later." She slept in the hotel during the ceremony and arranged to meet her boyfriend at the reception later.

Most frustrating is that the longer it takes her to fall asleep at night, the more she worries and the harder it becomes for her to

Figure 3.1 An estimated 10 percent of Americans struggle with chronic insomnia. © *Karen Winton/iStockphoto Inc.*

fall asleep. Alissa's doctor says she has insomnia, and Alissa is now being treated for the disorder.

From the Latin words *no* and *somnus*, insomnia literally means "no sleep." According to the American Academy of Sleep Medicine, one-third of adults in the United States experience insomnia, a disorder characterized by difficulty falling asleep, staying asleep, or waking up too early. It is estimated that about 10 percent of Americans struggle with insomnia chronically. Insomnia also appears to be more common among women, the poor, and seniors.[30]

Until recently, insomnia was believed to exist solely as a secondary symptom of another problem, such as a mental health or medical issue (now known as secondary insomnia). Since the mid-1990s, however, insomnia has been recognized as possibly being a disorder unto itself, and in such cases is referred to as primary insomnia. According to the American Academy of Sleep Medicine, insomnia may also be referred to as nonorganic, organic, or **idiopathic**. Nonorganic insomnia is most likely caused by an underlying mental health disorder, psychological factor, or sleep disruptive behaviors. Organic insomnia is likely caused by a medical disorder, physical condition, or substance exposure, but the specific cause remains unclear. Idiopathic insomnia refers to a lifelong sleep disorder, which starts as an infant or child and continues as an adult; cannot be explained by other causes; and is not a result of other sleep disorders, medical problems, psychiatric disorders, stressful events, medication use, or other behaviors.

SECONDARY INSOMNIA

Secondary insomnia can be triggered by an emotional, environmental, neurological, or other medical disorder, or by another sleep disorder. It often resolves itself with time or behavioral adjustments. Reasons for secondary insomnia include certain illnesses, such as some heart and lung diseases; pain; psychological conditions such as anxiety and depression; medicines that delay or disrupt sleep as a side effect, including certain asthma, allergy, and cold medicines and beta blockers; caffeine, nicotine, alcohol, and other substances that affect sleep; another sleep disorder, such as restless legs syndrome; a poor sleep environment, such as too much light, heat, or noise; or a change in sleep routine, due to a new baby or temporary illness such as the flu, for example.

PRIMARY INSOMNIA

Some experts think people with primary insomnia may be born with a greater chance of having it, and research is being conducted to explore the family link. A number of life changes can trigger primary insomnia, too, including major or long-lasting stress and emotional upset, such as a death in the family, a divorce, or job loss. Traveling extensively and to new time zones, as well as night-shift work, can also alter sleep patterns and lead to primary insomnia.

Even after a stressful life event passes, the insomnia might stick around. Insomnia woes may persist because of habits formed during the initial stressful period or busy travel time. Habits that may alter healthy night sleep include taking naps, worrying about sleep, or going to bed too early.

Sleep deprivation can occur with insomnia, leading to **excessive daytime sleepiness** and a lack of energy. All types of insomnia can cause those afflicted to feel depressed or irritable over time. A person may have trouble paying attention, learning, and remembering things. As in Alissa's case, it can impact your social life, limiting the energy you have for activities with friends and family.

A FAMILY AFFAIR?

Just like diabetes and heart disease, sleep troubles may run in families. A study in the December 2007 issue of the journal *Sleep* reported that people who have experienced bouts of insomnia are more likely to have a parent or sibling with the condition. In the largest study up to that time to evaluate the link between insomnia and familial ties, 953 adults between the ages of 18 and 83 were surveyed multiple times about their sleep habits as well as those of immediate family members. A little more than half of the survey-takers were classified as good sleepers—never reporting insomnia symptoms—while 32.5 percent experienced occasional symptoms, and 15.5 met all the criteria for the disorder.[31]

Study co-author Simon Beaulieu-Bonneau at Université Laval in Québec, Canada, says the subjects who experienced past and current stints of insomnia were significantly more likely than good sleepers (39.1 percent vs. 29 percent) to report that one or more family members had had nighttime problems.[32]

The question the researchers would like to answer is whether genetics or poor familial bedtime habits are at the root of insomnia. Experts say it could be a bit of both. "There is some evidence, from smaller studies, like one that looked at twins, that suggests a genetic factor," says Matthew Ebben, professor of neurology and neurobiology at Weill Cornell Medical College.[33] But according to study co-author Beaulieu-Bonneau, "We can't say for sure if it's either a genetic component or an environmental influence. We are still far from identifying a clear genetic marker for insomnia. But there might be a learned insomnia effect. People with bad sleep habits tend to transmit them to their children." He says this study supports the need for more research.[34]

DIAGNOSIS

Insomnia is typically diagnosed by a primary care physician, who will evaluate a patient's medical history and sleep history and conduct a physical exam. The physician may send the patient to a sleep center for a sleep study if he or she is unable to pinpoint the cause of the insomnia.

A sleep center specialist, often a psychologist or psychiatrist with special training in diagnosing and treating sleep disorders, will ask the patient whether they have any new or ongoing health problems, painful injuries or health conditions (such as arthritis), or are taking any over-the-counter or prescription medications.

He or she will want to hear about work or down-time habits that might be influencing the patient's insomnia, including exercise routines, use of caffeine, tobacco, or alcohol, and travel

What's Your Sleep History?

Sleep center doctors will also ask questions to help determine the patient's sleep history and why he may be experiencing insomnia. If a patient has a sleep partner, it may be handy to have him or her come along to help answer these queries:

- How often do you have trouble sleeping and how long has the problem has persisted?
- When do you go to bed and when do you get up on workdays and days off?
- How long does it take you to fall asleep and how often do you wake up at night?
- If you wake in the middle of the night, how long does it take to fall back asleep?
- Do you snore loudly and frequently, or wake up gasping or feeling out of breath?
- How refreshed do you feel when you wake up? How tired are you during the day?
- Do you doze off or have trouble staying awake during routine daytime tasks? Do you ever nod off while driving?
- Do you worry about falling asleep, staying asleep, or getting enough sleep?
- What do you eat or drink before bed, and do you take medicines before going to bed?
- What's your pre-bedtime routine?
- What are the noise level, lighting, and temperature like where you sleep?
- Do you have a TV or computer in your bedroom?

schedule. To obtain a better sense of a patient's sleep patterns and bedtime habits, the sleep center specialist may ask the patient to keep a sleep diary for a week or longer. This helps health experts determine which lifestyle patterns may be influencing sleepless nights.

A sleep center expert may also wish to conduct a polysomnogram (PSG), a test that records a patient's breathing, movements, heart function, and brain activity during sleep. For this study, the patient sleeps overnight at a sleep center. If the doctor suspects insomnia is caused by another sleep disorder, such as sleep apnea or restless legs syndrome, he will most likely request this test.

TREATMENT

Treatments for insomnia may include any number of techniques, including making small lifestyle changes. For some insomniacs, solving sleep problems may be as simple as cutting out a cup of coffee at night, or moving an exercise routine from the evening to the morning. Your doctor may suggest you pay bills at your lunch hour instead of before bed, or take up yoga, meditation, or other relaxation techniques.

Environmental changes may be also suggested. Parents of children with insomnia are often asked to remove stimulating objects from the bedroom, such as piles of stuffed animals, toys, the television, and the computer. Some people are under the impression that a very warm room helps induce sleep, but the body is actually more likely to fall asleep in a comfortably cool room.

According to a study published in 2005 in the medical journal *Sleep*, individuals with early-morning awakening insomnia experienced significantly improved sleep patterns following only two nights of bright-light therapy exposure. The study

Figure 3.2 Studies indicate that those suffering from early-morning awakening insomnia benefit from bright-light therapy. © *Scientifica/ Visuals Unlimited*

results showed that four hours of bright-light therapy for two consecutive nights produced a two-hour delay of the circadian phases of body temperature and melatonin rhythm in otherwise healthy adults with early-morning awakening insomnia. Over a four-week follow-up period, study subjects experienced a greater reduction of time awake after falling asleep, a trend toward waking up later in the morning, and more total sleep time compared with a control group that received only dim red-light exposure. Leon Lack, Ph.D., of Flinders University in Adelaide, Australia, and his colleagues found that the insomniacs who underwent bright-light therapy also showed more improvements in daytime functioning, including fewer days of feeling depressed.[35]

Counseling to help reduce anxiety and stress may also help in treating insomnia. Many sleep experts with psychology and psychiatry degrees use a form of therapy called **cognitive-behavioral therapy** to treat insomnia. CBT has been found to be as effective as prescription medicine for many types of insomnia. Its goal is to target the thoughts and actions that can disrupt a person's sleep. Besides encouraging good sleep habits, called good **sleep hygiene**, this type of therapy may use several methods to relieve sleep anxieties. Cognitive-behavioral therapy may offer better long-term relief than medicine alone, say many sleep experts.

Studies published in the *Journal of the American Medical Association* and *Archives of Internal Medicine* that compared CBT to popular prescription sleeping pills (of which 49 million prescriptions were dispensed in 2006) showed that CBT was more effective long-term in helping patients get

Famous Insomniacs

Not even the rich and famous are immune to sleepless nights. Some well-known individuals who claimed to have sleeping troubles include:

- **Winston Churchill, politician**
- **Thomas Edison, inventor**
- **Mark Twain, writer**
- **Franz Kafka, writer**
- **Groucho Marx, comic actor**
- **Judy Garland, entertainer**
- **Heath Ledger, actor**

rest. "There's a place for drugs short-term. But many people end up using them for a lifetime—that's not healthy," says Phil Gehrman, clinical associate professor of medicine and psychiatry at University of Pennsylvania Medical School in Philadelphia.[36]

A physician can give patients interested in trying CBT a referral to one of the 200-plus sleep clinics around the country that offer it. Most insurance plans should cover or partially cover treatment. There are also self-directed programs online that charge a small fee. Check with your doctor if you wish to use an online program, to make sure it is a safe, qualified resource.

DRUGS FOR INSOMNIA

Primary care physicians may prescribe a sleeping pill right off the bat to help get a patient through a bout of short-term insomnia, but many sleep specialists say drugs should only be used as a last resort. Some insomnia drugs help you fall asleep, but can leave some people feeling unrefreshed or groggy in the morning. In rare cases, they may even cause night-eating and night-driving that a patient does not recall doing in the morning. The U.S. Food and Drug Administration (FDA)—the federal agency that governs the trade and safety of food and drugs—has not approved all insomnia medicines for continuous, long-term use. A doctor can help insomniacs understand the benefits and potential problems of sleep medications.

Some people use natural remedies to treat their insomnia. These include melatonin and L-tryptophan supplements or **valerian** teas and extracts. These over-the-counter treatments are not regulated by the FDA. Because natural supplements can vary in purity from product to product, their safety and effectiveness is not well documented or understood.

Figure 3.3 Many sleep specialists say drugs should only be used as a last resort and always with close physician monitoring. © *Spauln/iStockphoto Inc.*

Insomniacs should always check with their doctor before taking any sleep medications. He or she can make sure the pills won't interact with other medications or with an existing medical condition. A doctor can also help a person determine the best dosage or alternatives to drugs. If a person does take a sleep medication, it should never be taken with alcohol. All side effects, such as dizziness or grogginess, should be reported to a physician immediately.

Sleep Apnea

Don used to snore so loudly that his six children, who slept in bedrooms one floor above their parent's bedroom, could hear him "sawing wood" at night. "He'd snore up a storm and then every so often he'd startle himself awake, choking and gasping for a breath," says Georgie, his wife of 45 years. She says he would immediately fall back to sleep and repeat the pattern all over again. "It would go on like that all night long," says Georgie, who had to sleep in another room if she wanted to get a good night's rest. It was literally decades later, when Don was in his 70s, that he was diagnosed with obstructive sleep apnea.

Sleep apnea is fairly common. More than 12 million Americans are affected by it, according to the National Institutes of Health. To give a comparison, about the same number of people have adult diabetes. Half of apnea sufferers are overweight and most snore heavily. There are two kinds of sleep apnea: **obstructive sleep apnea (OSA)** and **central sleep apnea**. On occasion, a physician will diagnose both forms in a patient and will refer to the condition as **mixed sleep apnea**. Much of this chapter will focus on OSA, because it is much more common than the other two types.

OBSTRUCTIVE SLEEP APNEA
Obstructive sleep apnea is a sleep-related breathing disorder that occurs when the muscle tissue in the back of a person's

throat relaxes and collapses, temporarily blocking the airway. This keeps air from getting to the lungs for 10 seconds or more, in some cases lasting more than a minute, until red flags start going up in the oxygen-deprived brain. That's when the brain sends signals to the apnea sleeper to wake up and breathe.

Blockage of the airway can happen a few times every hour, or literally hundreds of times per night. Many factors play into how frequently a person experiences sleep apnea episodes, including sleep position, weight, and whether the individual is taking medications, smokes, or has been drinking alcohol. The lapses in breathing can last a minute or longer. They can be frightening for a sleeping partner or household member who may witness the sleeper choking and struggling for air while asleep, or worse, temporarily not breathing.

CENTRAL AND MIXED SLEEP APNEA

Central sleep apnea is rare. It occurs when the airway is not blocked but the brain fails to signal the muscles to breathe because there is an underlying problem with the nerves that control breathing. In central apnea there is no effort to breathe at all for brief periods. Snoring does not typically occur in central apnea because of this complete cessation of breathing.

Mixed sleep apnea is a combination of the two other forms of the disorder in which there is blockage of the air passage and brain dysfunction. With each pause in breathing, the brain briefly arouses a person with sleep apnea in order for them to resume breathing. Despite the fact that a person never becomes totally alert, their sleep is extremely fragmented and of poor quality.

WHO GETS SLEEP APNEA?

Anyone can suffer from sleep apnea, at any age, but it is most common in men, and especially obese middle-aged men. One

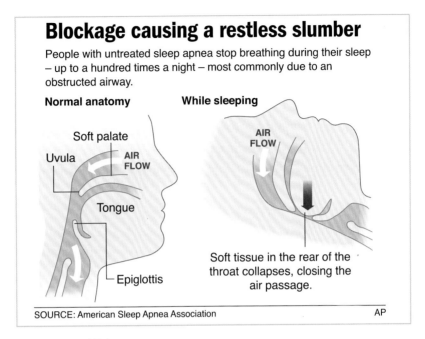

Blockage causing a restless slumber

People with untreated sleep apnea stop breathing during their sleep – up to a hundred times a night – most commonly due to an obstructed airway.

Normal anatomy

Soft palate

Uvula

AIR FLOW

Tongue

Epiglottis

While sleeping

AIR FLOW

Soft tissue in the rear of the throat collapses, closing the air passage.

SOURCE: American Sleep Apnea Association   AP

Figure 4.1 *AP Images*

out of 25 middle-aged men and 1 out of 50 middle-aged women have this disorder.

There is a strong relationship between weight and obstructive sleep apnea. Your neck gets thicker as you gain weight, and this increases the level of fat in the back of the throat, narrowing the airway. The more fat in the throat, the more likely the airway is to become blocked. Therefore, one of the first lines of treatment for overweight OSA sufferers is weight loss.

Sleep apnea is more common in African Americans, Hispanics, and Pacific Islanders than in Caucasians. If someone in your family has sleep apnea, you are more likely to develop it than someone without a family history of the condition. Those who live at high altitudes may also develop apnea.

People with smaller jaw structures may also be more prone to OSA. Children with larger tonsils may also have a greater chance of experiencing OSA. Medical conditions that can play a role in OSA include menopause, endocrine disorders such hypothryoidism and acromegaly, asthma, epilepsy, Down syndrome (in adults), enlarged tonsils and adenoids (especially in children), and history of a deviated septum or broken nose. People who get frequent sinus infections, have a lot of congestion in their airways (asthma), and those who suffer from hay fever also may be more prone.

SYMPTOMS

A household member or sleepmate may be able to tell you if you snore, but other daytime symptoms indicative of undiagnosed sleep apnea include snoring, gasping and choking at night, unintentional dozing off during the day, daytime grogginess and sleepiness, feeling unrefreshed and unrested upon waking in the morning, chronic fatigue, insomnia, and dozing off while driving. Additional signs of sleep apnea may include morning headaches, memory or learning problems, irritability, inability to concentrate, mood swings, personality changes, depression, dry mouth/throat, and frequent urination during the night.

Sleep apnea patient Liz Johns, 54, of Anadarko, Oklahoma, says that before she was diagnosed and treated for sleep apnea, she regularly had dreams that she was drowning or choking. "I would wake up gasping for air, my heart racing, my head sweaty," says Johns.[37]

Almost all people with OSA snore loudly (though people with central sleep apnea do not)—snoring is a sign that your airway is being partially blocked. Many apnea patients don't believe it when family members and friends claim they snore. One way to check is to tape record yourself as you sleep.

Often, people with OSA are groggy or tired during the day—even after taking a nap. That's because when you stop breathing or struggle with periods of airway resistance during sleep, your body wakes up, even if it's just for a few seconds and you are not aware of it. These apnea episodes disrupt your natural sleep cycles and cause you to move out of deep sleep and into light sleep several times during the night, resulting in poor sleep quality.

Sleep apnea is considered a serious disorder that needs to be treated by a medical professional. Untreated sleep apnea can increase the chance of having high blood pressure, heart attack, and stroke. Untreated sleep apnea can also increase the risk of diabetes and the risk for work-related accidents and driving accidents.

It's difficult to understand sleep apnea because you can't see it by day, you don't hear yourself snoring at night, and you

Do You Have an Undiagnosed Sleep Disorder?

Answer the following questions and learn whether you need to speak with your doctor about a potential sleep problem.

1. Do you snore at night, or do family members or roommates say you snore?

2. Do you experience breathing pauses during sleep that wake you up or that others notice?

3. Do you have trouble going to sleep at night, sleeping through the night, or waking too early?

4. Do you have difficulty staying awake during the day?

5. Are you groggy during the day? Have you experienced an unexplained decrease in daytime performance—physical, mental, or both?

If you answered yes to one or more of the above questions, check with your doctor to see if you may have a sleep disorder.

can't easily look inside your throat to check for abnormalities. So what might be happening in there that causes a partial or total block of your nightly supply of oxygen? Your throat muscles and tongue might be relaxing more than normal, or your tonsils and adenoids may be larger than normal. Or, the shape of your head and neck (termed "bony structure") and your airway size in the mouth and throat areas may be somewhat smaller than normal. If you are overweight, it is possible that the extra soft tissue in your throat makes it harder to keep the throat area open.

DIAGNOSING SLEEP APNEA

If your doctor refers you to a sleep specialist, the specialist will want to know about your symptoms and how long you have had them. As part of the exam, the doctor will check your mouth, nose, and throat for extra or large tissues. He'll view your tonsils, uvula (the tissue that hangs from the middle of the back of the mouth), and soft palate (the roof of your mouth in the back of your throat). He will also want to know if your symptoms began when you gained weight or stopped exercising.

Do a little medical homework: Collect information about your sleeping self from those who sleep with you or have seen you sleep, including a spouse, relative, friends, teammates, and roommates. The sleep doctor may ask you to keep a sleep diary for a few weeks. In the diary, you log when you go to sleep, when you wake, and how you feel upon waking. You can also jot down bedtime routines and daily activities or behaviors your doctor should know about, such as smoking and drinking habits, and any medicines you might take for allergies, asthma, heart disease, psychological conditions, or other conditions.

If a doctor suspects sleep apnea, he or she will order an overnight sleep study called a polysomnogram (PSG), which records numerous body functions. To take this test, you have to go to a

Home Tests

Many people do not relish the idea of spending a night in a sleep clinic hooked up to all sorts of monitoring equipment. More recently, home tests have been made available that may help diagnose sleep apnea. They are called "oximetry" tests because they monitor oxygen levels while you sleep. There is, however, some question as to the reliability of these tests, which can be obtained only from a doctor. Not all insurance companies are willing to cover such testing. They should not be used as the sole screening tool for apnea, because they may produce a false normal diagnosis, says psychiatrist Carlos Schenck in his book *Sleep: A Groundbreaking Guide to the Mysteries, the Problems, and the Solutions* (Avery, 2008).

sleep center—there are a thousand in the United States—staffed with doctors and others who specialize in sleep medicine. While you sleep, they monitor your physical state, tracking your brain waves, and heart beat. The test will record muscle movements and can detect how serious your sleep apnea may be.

Sometimes a second polysomnogram is required if doctors suspect OSA because they may wish to give you a **continuous positive airway pressure (CPAP)** treatment as you sleep—or CPAP study. A CPAP device helps apnea patients breathe better at night. By observing you asleep with the CPAP on, they can figure out exactly how much air pressure you require in order to receive proper oxygen.

Once you have completed your tests, the sleep medicine specialist will review the results and work with you and your family to create a treatment plan. Sometimes you will consult with other specialists, too, if your apnea is linked to other health problems.

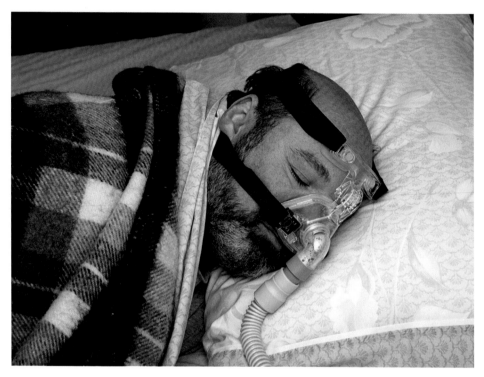

Figure 4.2 A CPAP device may help apnea patients breathe better at night.
© Howard Sandler/iStockphoto Inc.

If you suspect you have a sleep disorder and your doctor has never brought it up, do not be shy about suggesting a visit to a sleep lab. Apnea patient Liz Johns says it was her idea to have a polysomnogram performed, not her doctor's. After decades of poor sleep and serious daytime fatigue, the 54-year-old working mom did her own research on the Internet, which led her to suspect her health problems were sleep-focused. When she brought it up with her doctor, he was more than happy to refer her to the nearest sleep lab, where she was diagnosed with obstructive sleep apnea and treated. She now rejoices in well-rested nights and newfound energy by day.[38]

TREATMENT

Medical devices, behavioral modification, and surgery are among the ways doctors treat apnea patients. Continuous positive airway pressure, the most common treatment for OSA sufferers, is delivered via a device worn over the nose or face. The device produces air that gently blows into the back of the throat, maintaining an open airway while you sleep. The amount of air pressure needed is different for each person. A CPAP study will show what level is just right for a patient and help the physician prescribe the proper breathing apparatus. Patients require a prescription for CPAP and can order one from a distributor of **pulmonary** devices. Some patients worry that the device will be a burden or unattractive to their sleeping partners. Once they use it, however, they realize the benefits—a refreshing sleep, no more snoring, a happier patient by day—are worth it. "My husband did not care how the equipment looked. He was just thrilled I wasn't snoring anymore and glad that I feel great again—like my old self," says sleep apnea patient Liz Johns. Johns, who always felt groggy during waking hours and drank numerous cups of coffee to ward off chronic fatigue every day, believes she had sleep apnea for a decade before she read about it online and asked her physician to send her for a sleep test.[39]

Behavioral modifications to treat OSA include weight loss, sleep positioning, and a simple oral appliance worn during sleep. Weight loss can help overweight people with OSA decrease the amount of fat that may be obstructing their throat. Dropping a few pounds may even stop apnea symptoms altogether. Position therapy encourages patients to sleep off of their backs. Some patients tilt up the head of the bed by placing bricks under the head end. An oral appliance, much like a mouth guard used during sports, may help position the jaw better and keep the airway open, reducing apnea symptoms.

(Continues on page 50)

Behind the Quiet Door of a Sleep Center

When Meg and John were pregnant with their first child, they would always pass by the low-lit, quiet entrance to their hospital's sleep lab on the way to Meg's obstetrician's office. They would make jokes about the secret goings-ons behind the lab's front door, and in his effort to relax his wife on the way to her appointment, John would kid around that they should make a lot of noise and wake the sleepers up. Four years later, the sleep lab wasn't quite as funny to John as he found himself walking through the lab's doors hoping the sleep doctors there could uncover the answer to why he snored so much at night and awoke feeling unrested and cranky each morning.

At the center, John first had a consultation with a sleep specialist who asked questions about his sleep habits and health history, as well as his family medical history and daytime routines. He was also asked to keep a log for a few weeks to help the sleep specialist better understand his day-to-day mood and activities, including work and family logistics, stress level, exercise, meals, caffeine intake, what time he went to sleep and woke up, and other details.

Leaving their toddler with his grandmother, Meg had come along with John at the sleep specialist's request to help add details about John's nocturnal symptoms—things she noticed while John slept, like the choking sounds he sometimes made, his small lapses in breath, and his brief awakenings.

John was asked to make a second visit, at which time a team of technicians and doctors monitored him while he slept all night. Before dozing off, a technician placed small electrodes on his head and body to record bodily activities such as brain wave function, breathing rate, heart rate, temperature, muscle movement, and eye movements. This painless test is called a polysomnogram, and though the sensors were placed on him when he was awake, the rest of the monitoring took place while John slept. (Children may undergo polysomnograms too. A parent or guardian stays in the same room as the child sleeps.)

Sleep centers, also called sleep labs, are dedicated to diagnosing patients such as John who have sleep-related problems. There are 1,500 of them scattered across the United States and accredited by the American Academy of Sleep Medicine. Many hospitals and medical centers support such centers.

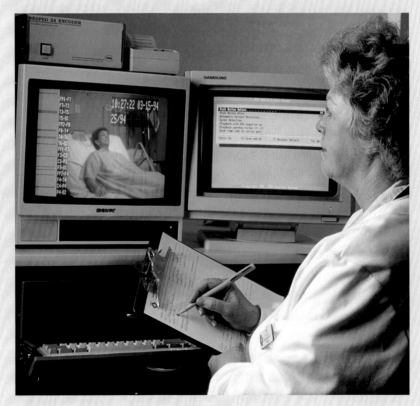

Figure 4.3 A researcher uses a television screen to remotely observe a woman during research into sleep disorders. © Ed Young/Photo Researchers, Inc.

(Continued from page 47)

Several types of surgery exist for the treatment of OSA. Uvulopalatopharyngoplasty, or UPPP, enlarges the airway by removing or shortening the uvula (tissue that hangs at the back of the roof of the mouth) as well as removing the tonsils, adenoids, and part of the soft palate. This surgery is not effective for all apnea patients. According to the American Academy of Sleep Medicine, the efficacy of UPPP surgery was 40.7 percent in 1996. Tracheostomy is used only in cases of severe sleep apnea. A small hole is made in the windpipe (trachea) and a tube inserted, which allows air to flow through the tube and into the lungs. This surgery is very successful but is needed only in patients not responding to all other possible treatments. Other possible surgeries for some people with sleep apnea include rebuilding the lower jaw, surgery on the nose, and surgery to treat obesity.

Before considering surgery, an X ray, **CT scan**, or **MRI** of the facial-skeletal area may be worth considering to get a clear picture of exactly what is happening structurally. Nasopharyngoscopy, which allows for a direct exam of the upper airway from nose to larynx, is also warranted, as well as a second opinion from an expert at a major medical center.

Movement Disorders

Many a couple have been forced to sleep separately because of a partner with a sleep movement disorder. Not only do movement disorders wreak havoc on relationships, but they typically leave sufferers feeling fatigued, sore, and moody by day.

PERIODIC LIMB MOVEMENT DISORDER (PLMD)

Periodic limb movement disorder, once referred to as nocturnal myoclonus, is characterized by repetitive, stereotyped movements of the limbs. PLMD, also referred to as PLM, often occurs in the legs, involving flexing of the big toe, ankle, knee, and hip, but in some people the upper extremities are involved. Limb movements, such as kicking and flexing, occur most frequently during light non-REM sleep and are separated by regular intervals of 5 to 90 seconds each. PLMD sufferers experience intermittent leg movements during the night—spasms that can last between 20 and 40 seconds at a time. The constant, repetitive movements disrupt normal sleep patterns and can lead to insomnia and daytime struggles, including reduced productivity at work, social problems, and reduced energy levels.

PLMD does not seem to be gender specific, and it can affect young and old alike, though it appears to be more common in the elderly. According to the National Sleep Foundation, about 45 percent of the elderly have some form of PLMD. The

Figure 5.1 In periodic limb movement disorder, repetitive limb movements disrupt normal sleep patterns and can lead to insomnia and daytime struggles. © *Carol and Mike Werner/Phototake*

disruptions cause nighttime insomnia and leave patients fatigued and sleepy during the day.[40]

Some medical conditions are associated with PLMD, including kidney failure, diabetes, **anemia** (iron deficiency), and spinal cord injury. PLMD is common in patients with narcolepsy and REM sleep behavior disorder.

The exact cause of periodic limb movement disorder isn't understood. Certain medications, however, are known to make the condition worse, and include some antidepressants, antihistamines, and some antipsychotics. PLMD may involve altered central **dopamine** mechanisms, since dopaminergic agents or other drugs that interact with dopamine mechanisms (such as **opiates**) effectively treat most patients with the disorder. Dopamine is a chemical messenger responsible for transmitting signals between one area of the brain, the substantia nigra, and the next relay station of the brain, the corpus striatum, to produce smooth, purposeful muscle activity.

During sleep tests, abnormal limb movements have been associated with physiological arousal in autonomic or cortical functioning, suggesting that PLMD may be part of an underlying arousal disorder (arousal disorders include **parasomnias** such as sleepwalking and night terrors).[41]

Some individuals exhibit periodic limb movements during sleep that do not arouse them and disturb normal sleep cycles. This is referred to as periodic limb movements of sleep and uses a similar acronym, PLMS. Controversy exists about the clinical significance of periodic limb movements during sleep when complaints of symptoms do not exist.

Diagnosing PLMD

If a person or a family member suspects PLMD, a family physician or sleep specialist should examine him. A clinical history as well as an overnight polysomnogram (PSG) conducted at a sleep lab should be conducted, and a complete neurological exam is also recommended. Respiratory monitoring during the PSG should be performed to rule out other sleep disorders.

Treatment

Before treating PLMD pharmacologically, a patient's medications should be analyzed to be sure he is not taking drugs that may be causing PLMD. Treatment options for PLMD include dopaminergic agents, sedative/hypnotic drugs, and anticonvulsant medications.

Dopaminergic agents, typically used to treat Parkinson's disease, have been shown to reduce symptoms of PLMD and are considered the initial treatment of choice. Short-term results of treatment with dopaminergic agents levodopa plus carbidopa have been reported, although most patients eventually will develop augmentation, which means that symptoms are reduced at night but begin to develop earlier in the day than usual. Another category of dopaminergic agents are **dopamine agonists**. Agonists alter the activity of dopamine receptors in the brain. Examples of dopamine agonists are pramipexole and ropinirole hydrochloride. They may be effective in some patients and are less likely to cause augmentation.

Drugs known as **benzodiazepines** (such as clonazepam [Klonapin] and diazepam [Valium]) are sometimes prescribed to help patients sleep more restfully. They also have side effects, such as sleepiness during the day. These medications should not be used in apnea patients since they can induce or aggravate that condition. For more severe PLMD symptoms, opioids such as codeine, propoxyphene, or oxycodone may be prescribed. **Anticonvulsants** such as carbamazepine and gabapentin are also used in severe cases of PLMD to suppress the muscle contractions associated with the disorder.

The Future of PLMD

Animal and imaging studies have explored and continue to investigate the etiology, neuropathology, and physiology of PLMD. Identifying the genes at play in the condition and tracking the nocturnal habits and daytime sleepiness of more children and adults with this condition will help scientists better understand how to develop treatments. More research into the role of altered central dopaminergic mechanisms in animals and humans will also lead to better understanding and treatment options. What's more, additional large multicenter studies need to take place in order to assess the quality of life in patients with PLMD who take dopamine agonists, opioids, and anticonvulsants for their symptoms.[42]

RESTLESS LEGS SYNDROME

Restless legs syndrome (RLS) is a **neurological disorder** that causes an almost irresistible urge to move the legs. The urge to move is usually due to unpleasant feelings in the legs when a person is asleep or resting. Though RLS is not limited to the hours when a person sleeps, it is technically not a sleep disorder, yet it often causes sleep disruption and so is included here.

RLS patients have described the feelings in their limbs as creeping, burning, or tingling sensations. Doctors may use the terms *paresthesias* (abnormal sensations) or *dysesthesias* (unpleasant abnormal sensations) for the feelings one gets with RLS. These sensations can range in severity from uncomfortable to irritating to painful. They tend to lessen or disappear when a person moves. RLS sufferers may pace the floor and toss and turn in bed.

Primary, or idiopathic, RLS is the most common type of the condition. Its cause is not understood. Primary RLS, once it begins, usually becomes a lifelong condition. Over time, symptoms tend to get worse and occur more often, especially if they began in childhood or early in adult life. In milder cases, there may be long periods of time with no symptoms, or symptoms may last only for short stretches.

Secondary RLS is a symptom of another condition, or sometimes caused by medications. This type of RLS will disappear when the associated condition improves or the medicine is discontinued.

RLS can make it hard to fall asleep and stay asleep. Like those who suffer from sleep apnea and narcolepsy, RLS patients tend to feel tired and sleepy during the day because their nights are filled with poor-quality sleep or not enough sleep. Work, family life, and social activities take a toll. Depression and mood swings may occur.

The severity of RLS depends on the regularity and intensity of symptoms, daytime sleepiness factor, amount of discomfort in the legs and arms, amount of relief obtained from moving limbs, how much sleep disturbance one experiences, mood and how often one feels angry, depressed, sad, anxious, or irritable. RLS symptoms often improve with medical treatment. Some patients have remissions—days, weeks, or months when symptoms decline or disappear temporarily.

It is estimated that RLS affects as many as 12 million Americans, but the actual number may be higher. Some sleep experts believe RLS is underdiagnosed, and in some cases misdiagnosed, for symptoms of anxiety, insomnia, aging, stress, arthritis, and muscle cramping. In children, RLS can be misdiagnosed as typical growing pains. The condition is more common in females. Middle-aged or older patients seem to be most affected, and symptoms tend to worsen with age and the passage of time. In rare instances, symptoms may spontaneously decrease. More than 80 percent of patients with restless legs syndrome also experience periodic limb movement disorder while sleeping, according to the National Institutes of Neurological Disorders and Stroke.

The cause of RLS is unknown, though research indicates that a family history exists in about half the cases, suggesting a genetic link. In nonfamily-linked cases, RLS may be related to low iron levels or anemia. Once iron levels are corrected with supplements and/or better nutrition, patients may see a reduction in symptoms. Chronic conditions, such as kidney failure, diabetes, Parkinson's disease, and peripheral **neuropathy** may also be linked to RLS. Some pregnant women experience RLS, especially in their last trimester, but symptoms tend to disappear within a month post-delivery. Finally, use of some medications may cause RLS, such as antinausea drugs (prochlorperazine or metoclopramide), antiseizure drugs (phenytoin or droperidol), and antipsychotic drugs (haloperidol or phenothiazine derivatives). Some cold and allergy medications may increase symptoms.

Diagnosing RLS

The four basic criteria for diagnosing RLS include a desire to move the limbs; symptoms that are worse or present only during rest and are partially or temporarily relieved by activity; motor restlessness; and nocturnal worsening of symptoms. Most people with RLS have sleep disturbances because of limb discomfort and movement that can cause excessive daytime sleepiness and fatigue. Physicians must take a thorough patient history, family health history, physical exam, and evaluation of current symptoms.

If a patient's history suggests RLS, sleep lab tests can help rule out other conditions. Blood tests to exclude anemia, decreased iron stores, diabetes, and renal dysfunction are recommended. Tests may also be conducted to measure electrical activity in muscles and nerves, and rule out other diseases of the nerves. Negative results from these tests may indicate a diagnosis of RLS.

Treatment

There is no cure yet for RLS. Current therapies, however, can ease symptoms and offer more restful nights. Movement brings relief to RLS patients, but it is usually only temporary. Patients who have RLS because of an underlying disease, such as diabetes, can often be treated by treating the primary disease. In patients with idiopathic RLS, however, treatment focuses on relieving symptoms.

Decreased use of caffeine, alcohol, and tobacco may provide relief. Iron, folate, and magnesium supplements may help in some. Studies suggest that sticking to a routine sleep schedule can reduce symptoms. Exercise, leg massage, hot or cold packs, and warm baths also help some patients, but total relief can be elusive.

Doctors may suggest medications to treat RLS, though no single drug is right for everyone since RLS sufferers experience varying degrees of symptoms. Generally, physicians choose from dopaminergics, benzodiazepines (**central nervous system** depressants), opioids, and anticonvulsants. In 2005, ropinirole became the only drug approved by the U.S. Food and Drug Administration specifically for the treatment of moderate to severe RLS. It has been FDA-approved for the treatment of Parkinson's disease since 1997.

The Future of RLS

The National Institute of Neurological Disorders and Stroke (NINDS), one of the National Institutes of Health, has the primary responsibility for conducting and supporting research on RLS. The goal of this research is to increase scientific understanding of RLS, find improved methods of diagnosing and treating the syndrome, and discover ways to prevent it. NINDS-supported researchers are investigating the possible role of dopamine function in RLS. Researchers suspect that impaired transmission of dopamine signals may play a role in RLS. Additional research should provide new information about how RLS occurs and may help investigators identify more successful treatment options.

Research on **pallidotomy**, a surgical procedure in which a portion of the brain called the globus pallidus is lesioned, may contribute to a greater understanding of RLS and treatment of the condition. One study by NINDS-funded researchers showed that a patient with RLS and Parkinson's disease benefited from a pallidotomy and obtained relief from the limb discomfort caused by RLS. Additional research must be conducted to learn whether pallidotomy would be effective in RLS patients who do not also have Parkinson's disease. In other related research, NINDS scientists are conducting studies with patients to better understand the physiological mechanisms of PLMD associated with RLS.

OTHER MOVEMENT-RELATED SLEEP DISORDERS

Sleep starts, also called hypnic or **hypnagogic** jerks, are common as people fall asleep. Most people at one time or another have experienced a sudden jerk or start just as they are drifting off at night. In some instances, however, a person may have strong or frequent contractions of the muscles in their legs, arm, or head, which can lead to insomnia.

Some infants of 12 months or younger may experience **rhythmic movement disorder**, characterized by a group of repeated movements (usually in the head and neck) which occur right before sleep, according Stanford sleep expert William Dement, in his book *The Promise of Sleep* (Dell, 2000). The child may lie down or sit up and repeatedly "bang" his or her head against a wall or headboard, and is sometimes accompanied by rolling or rocking. It is often referred to as "head banging" and is disturbing for parents to witness; however, most children outgrow it.

Nocturnal leg cramps are exactly what they sound like. A sleeper may describe them as "a Charlie horse" in his or her calf muscles, and may awake with very sore calves the next day. Runners complain of such experiences, which can be strong enough to waken them in the night. They may last just a few seconds or half a minute. Their cause is not well understood.

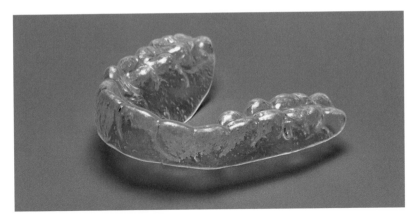

Figure 5.2 A mouthguard can protect against the effects of tooth grinding, also known as bruxism. © *BSIP/Phototake*

Tooth grinding and clenching of the jaw during sleep is known as **bruxism**. This disorder is common in adults and has been linked to stress, anxiety, and depression. In some patients, it can be so severe that it wears down or causes cracked teeth. Jaw pain and tightness, worn tooth enamel, a dull morning headache, earache, chronic facial pain, and popping, clicking, and locking of the jaw can also be symptoms. Bruxism can lead to disorders of the temporomandibular joint (TMJ), located on both sides of the head where the lower jawbone meets the skull. Some antidepressants, such as sertraline (Zoloft) and fluoxetine (Prozac), medications used to treat anxiety and depression, can themselves cause bruxism as a side effect.[43]

Tips for beating bruxism include the use of a special mouth guard during sleep. Applying warm compresses to the jaw area may help alleviate aching associated with bruxism. Cutting out gum, caffeine, and crunchy and chewy foods (such as bagels) can help, too. Consciously keeping one's teeth apart during the day and letting your tongue rest gently between the upper and lower teeth will help remind you not to clench. If symptoms such as headache, facial, jaw, neck, or ear pain persists, a visit to the dentist is recommended.

Narcolepsy

Tim and Gina had been married only a few months when Gina noticed that every time they visited her parents for dinner, Tim would fall asleep at the table. Gina often felt angry on the drive home, telling Tim she was afraid her parents thought they were boring him. It wasn't until Tim's office picnic the following summer when Gina overheard the other young lawyers in his firm teasing Tim about how he nodded off in meetings and in court sometimes that she recalled times when they were dating that he'd fall asleep during movies or appear groggy at parties. At the time, she had attributed his fatigue to the long hours he spent in law school classes and studying. A nurse, Gina now began to suspect a sleeping disorder. One week later, they walked out of Tim's physician's office with a referral to a sleep center recommending a multiple sleep latency test (MSLT), but a thorough medical history had Tim's doctor essentially convinced the final diagnosis would be narcolepsy.

Narcolepsy is a chronic neurological disorder. It is caused by the brain's inability to regulate sleep-wake cycles normally. People with narcolepsy experience fleeting urges to sleep throughout the day. If the urge becomes overwhelming, patients fall asleep for periods lasting from a few seconds to several minutes. In rare cases, some people may remain asleep for an hour or longer.

Narcoleptic sleep events can happen any time, any place, and can be profoundly disabling for people with the disorder. Sometimes narcoleptics involuntarily fall asleep at work or at school, while having a conversation, socializing, and eating. Narcolepsy can put a person at risk when he or she is driving or operating heavy equipment or dangerous machinery.

Narcolepsy is the third most common sleep disorder, after sleep apnea and restless legs syndrome, and it's the second leading cause of daytime sleepiness, after sleep apnea. It is estimated that about 1 out of every 2,000 Americans have narcolepsy.[44] Doctors believe many people suffer from this disorder, but are never diagnosed, or are diagnosed years down the road, when narcolepsy has already had a devastating impact on a person's life.

Narcolepsy appears to be indiscriminate and occurs in every part of the world, in all racial and ethnic groups. It seems to affect men and women equally, and children are not immune to it. Prevalence rates vary among populations. Compared to the U.S. population, for example, the prevalence rate is substantially lower in Israel (about one per 500,000) and considerably higher in Japan (about one per 600).[45]

SYMPTOMS

Symptoms of the condition usually appear during the teen years. A young person will be extremely tired much of the time. This can often be dismissed as a teen's need for extra sleep since he or she is still growing—or worse, as laziness (see Chapter 8 for more information on childhood narcolepsy). Those who are diagnosed with narcolepsy often do not learn about it for some time—possibly through years or decades of feeling groggy and exhausted. Sleepiness is not widely recognized as a symptom of a medical condition, so many narcoleptics wait a long time before they seek medical attention. Sadly, they usually wait until their symptoms are completely debilitating.

Figure 6.1 Excessive daytime sleepiness is a major symptom of narcolepsy. © Bill Crawford/iStockphoto Inc.

In addition to excessive daytime sleepiness (EDS), three other major symptoms often characterize narcolepsy: **cataplexy**, or the sudden loss of voluntary muscle control; vivid hallucinations during sleep onset or upon awakening; and brief episodes of paralysis at the beginning or end of sleep.

During hypnagogic hallucinations, patients experience dream-like auditory or visual hallucinations. These occur while patients are just beginning to doze off or just awaking.

Cataplexy involves a sudden episode of muscle weakness triggered by emotions. A patient's knees may buckle or give way when they laugh, or feel elation, surprise or anger. Their head may drop or their jaw may become slack. In severe cases of cataplexy, the patient might fall down and become paralyzed for a few minutes. Reflexes are useless during an attack.

Narcoleptics have a reputation for sleeping constantly, and sleeping much longer than others, but people with narcolepsy do not spend a substantially greater portion of each 24-hour period asleep than normal sleepers—their sleep is just broken up differently. Most narcoleptic patients don't just experience chronic fatigue and daytime naps; they also experience frequent awakenings during nighttime sleep. Because of this, narcolepsy

Doctors Dedicated to Narcolepsy

In the early 1970s, American physician and sleep pioneer Dr. William Dement founded the Stanford University Sleep Clinic. It was the first medical clinic ever established specializing in sleep disorders. Today, the clinic diagnoses and treats patients who have difficulties falling asleep or staying asleep at night, problems with excessive daytime fatigue, and other medical problems related to sleep.

The Stanford Center for Narcolepsy was established in the 1980s as part of the Department of Psychiatry and Behavioral Sciences. Today, it is a world leader in narcolepsy research. The Stanford Center for Narcolepsy was the first to report that narcolepsy-related cataplexy is caused by hypocretin (orexin) abnormalities in animal models and in humans.

Drs. Emmanuel Mignot and Seiji Nishino direct Stanford's Center for Narcolepsy, which treats several hundred patients with the disorder every year. Many of their patients participate in narcolepsy studies in order to help further understanding and treatment of the disorder. According to their Web site (http://med.stanford.edu/school/Psychiatry/narcolepsy), the center is always looking for volunteers to help further research. Patients is considered to be a disorder of the normal boundaries between the sleeping and waking states.

Scientists now believe that narcolepsy results from disease processes affecting brain mechanisms that regulate REM sleep. For normal sleepers, a typical sleep cycle is about 100–110 minutes long, beginning with NREM sleep and transitioning to REM sleep after 80–100 minutes. People with narcolepsy,

can participate in the following ways: genetic studies, drug clinical trials, hypocretin measurement studies in the cerebrospinal fluid, and functional MRI studies.

Figure 6.2 Dr. William Dement, founder of the Stanford University Sleep Clinic, the first of its kind in the United States. © *Ed Souza/ Stanford News Service*

however, frequently enter REM sleep within a few minutes of falling asleep.

HOW IS NARCOLEPSY DIAGNOSED?

Narcolepsy is not definitively diagnosed in most patients until 10 to 15 years after the first symptoms appear. The long lag-time is related to the fact that the disorder's subtle onset and the variability of symptoms make it hard to see right away. There is little public awareness of the condition, however, and few health professionals are trained to spot it. Furthermore, when symptoms initially develop, people often do not recognize that they are experiencing the onset of a distinct neurological disorder and thus fail to seek medical treatment.

If narcolepsy is suspected, a patient's primary care physician or the sleep expert he is referred to will conduct a clinical examination and an exhaustive medical history. These are essential for diagnosis and treatment. None of the major symptoms, however, is exclusive to narcolepsy. Excessive daytime sleepiness—the most common of all narcoleptic symptoms—can result from a wide range of medical conditions, including other sleep disorders such as sleep apnea, viral or bacterial infections, mood disorders such as depression and anxiety, and painful chronic illnesses such as congestive heart failure and rheumatoid arthritis that disrupt normal sleep patterns.

Some medications can also cause excessive daytime sleepiness, and so can caffeine, alcohol, and nicotine. Sleepiness from narcolepsy can also be confused with symptoms of sleep deprivation, which has become one of the most common causes of excessive daytime sleepiness among Americans.

Symptoms alone will not confirm an accurate diagnosis, so a battery of specialized tests, which can be performed in a sleep disorders clinic, is usually required before a diagnosis can be pinpointed. A polysomnogram (PSG) and the **multiple sleep latency test (MSLT)** are key to helping doctors determine whether a narcolepsy diagnosis is appropriate. As discussed in other sections of this book, the PSG is an overnight test that takes continuous multiple measurements while a patient is asleep, to document abnormalities in the sleep cycle. It records heart and respiratory rates, electrical activity in the brain through electroencephalography, and nerve activity in muscles through **electromyography**. A PSG can help reveal whether REM sleep occurs at abnormal times in the sleep cycle and can eliminate the possibility that an individual's symptoms result from another condition.

The MSLT is performed during the day to measure a person's tendency to fall asleep and to determine whether isolated elements of REM sleep intrude at inappropriate times during the waking hours. As part of the test, an individual is asked to take four or five short naps usually scheduled two hours apart over the course of a day. This test measures the amount of time it takes for a person to fall asleep. Because sleep latency periods are normally 10 minutes or longer, a latency period of five minutes or less is considered suggestive of narcolepsy. The MSLT also measures heart and respiratory rates, records nerve activity in muscles, and pinpoints the occurrence of abnormally timed REM episodes through EEG recordings. Healthy sleepers enter the first REM sleep cycle about 90 to 100 minutes after the onset of sleep. If a person enters REM sleep either at the beginning or within a few minutes of sleep onset during at least two of the scheduled naps, this is considered a positive indication of narcolepsy.

TREATMENT

There is no cure for narcolepsy, but the most disabling symptoms of the condition—excessive daytime sleepiness and cataplexy—can be controlled in most patients with medication. For decades, doctors have used central nervous system stimulants to help maintain a wakeful state. These drugs are classified as **amphetamines**, and include methylphenidate, dextroamphetamine, methamphetamine, and pemoline, which help alleviate EDS and reduce the incidence of sleep episodes during the day. For most patients these medications are effective at reducing daytime drowsiness and improving levels of alertness. These medications have a wide array of undesirable side effects, however, so they must be carefully monitored. Common side effects include irritability and nervousness, shakiness, disturbances in heart rhythm, stomach upset, nighttime sleep disruption, and anorexia. Patients may also develop tolerance with long-term use, leading to the need for increased dosages to maintain effectiveness. Doctors should be careful when prescribing these drugs and patients should be careful using them because the potential for abuse is high with any amphetamine.

In 1999, the FDA approved a new nonamphetamine, wakefulness-promoting medication called modafinil that treats EDS. In clinical trials, modafinil proved to be effective in alleviating EDS while producing fewer, less serious side effects than do amphetamines. Headache is the most commonly reported adverse effect. Long-term use of modafinil does not appear to lead to tolerance, but it may be habit-forming.

Two classes of antidepressant drugs have also proved effective in controlling cataplexy in many patients: **tricyclic antidepressants** (including imipramine, desipramine, clomipramine, and protriptyline) and **selective serotonin reuptake inhibitors** (including fluoxetine [Prozac] and sertraline [Zoloft]). In general, antidepressants produce fewer adverse effects than do amphetamines. Troublesome side effects still occur in some patients, however, including impotence, high blood pressure, and heart rhythm irregularities.

In 2002, the FDA approved Xyrem (sodium oxybate or gamma hydroxybutyrate, also known as GHB) for treating people with narcolepsy who experience episodes of cataplexy. Because of safety concerns associated with the use of this drug, the distribution of Xyrem is tightly restricted.

None of the above medications helps narcoleptics stay alert and avoid sleepiness all of the time, so sleep experts recommend that drug therapy be supplemented with behavioral modification strategies. Taking a short, regularly scheduled nap helps some patients reduce sleep attacks, and sometimes adults can negotiate with their employers for modified work schedules so they can take naps when necessary and perform their most demanding tasks when they are more alert. The **Americans with Disabilities Act** requires employers to provide reasonable accommodations for all employees with disabilities, and narcolepsy is considered a disability. Parents can work with teachers and coaches to help children and adolescents with narcolepsy. Modifying class schedules and informing school personnel of special needs, including medication requirements during the school day, all help ease a child's ability to cope with the disorder.

Better quality nighttime sleep can combat EDS and help relieve persistent feelings of fatigue. Ways to enhance sleep quality include maintaining a regular sleep schedule; avoiding alcohol and caffeine for several hours before bedtime; avoiding smoking, especially at night; maintaining a comfortable, adequately warmed bedroom environment; engaging in relaxing activities such as a warm bath before bedtime; and exercising for at least 20 minutes per day (beginning at least four or five hours before bedtime).

Safety precautions, particularly when driving, are of paramount importance for all persons with narcolepsy. Although the disorder, in itself, is not fatal, EDS and cataplexy can lead to serious injury or death if left uncontrolled. Suddenly falling asleep or losing muscle control can transform actions that are ordinarily safe, such as walking down a long flight of stairs, into hazards. People with untreated narcoleptic symptoms are involved in automobile accidents about 10 times more frequently than the general population. Accident rates, however, are normal among patients who have received appropriate medication.

Patient support groups can bolster a patient's ability to cope with narcolepsy and feel less isolated. Many patients attempt to avoid experiencing strong emotions, since humor, excitement, and other intense feelings can trigger cataplectic attacks. Because of the widespread lack of public knowledge about the disorder, people with narcolepsy are often unfairly judged to be lazy, unintelligent, undisciplined, or unmotivated. This type of stigmatization can increase the tendency toward self-imposed isolation. The empathy and understanding that support groups offer people can be crucial to their overall sense of well-being and provide them with a network of social contacts who can offer practical help and emotional support.

NARCOLEPSY RESEARCH

Within the federal government, the National Institute of Neurological Disorders and Stroke (NINDS), a component of the National Institutes of Health (NIH), has primary responsibility for sponsoring research on neurological disorders. As part of its mission, the NINDS supports research on narcolepsy and other sleep disorders with a neurological basis through grants to major medical institutions across the country.

Within the National Heart, Lung, and Blood Institute, also a component of the NIH, the National Center on Sleep Disorders Research (NCSDR) coordinates federal government sleep research activities and shares information with private and nonprofit groups. NCSDR staff also promote doctoral and post-doctoral training programs, and educate the public and health care professionals about sleep disorders.

NINDS-sponsored researchers are conducting studies devoted to further clarifying the range of genetic factors—both HLA genes and non-HLA genes—that may cause narcolepsy. Other scientists are conducting investigations using animal models to identify **neurotransmitters** other than the hypocretins that may contribute to disease development. A greater understanding of the complex genetic and biochemical bases of narcolepsy will eventually lead to the formulation of new therapies to control symptoms and may lead to a cure. Researchers are also investigating the modes of action of wake-fulness-promoting compounds to widen the range of available therapeutic options.

Scientists have long suspected that abnormal immunological processes may be an important element in the cause of narcolepsy, but until recently clear evidence supporting this suspicion has been lacking. NINDS-sponsored scientists have recently uncovered evidence demonstrating the presence of unusual, possibly pathological, forms of immunological activity in narcoleptic dogs. These researchers are investigating whether drugs that suppress immunological processes may interrupt the development of narcolepsy in this animal model.

Recently, there has been a growing awareness that narcolepsy can develop during childhood and may contribute to the development of behavior disorders. A group of NINDS-sponsored scientists is now conducting a large epidemiological study to determine the prevalence of narcolepsy in children ages 2 to 14 who have been diagnosed with attention-deficit/hyperactivity disorder.

Finally, the NINDS continues to support investigations into the basic biology of sleep, including the brain mechanisms involved in generating and regulating REM sleep. Scientists are examining physiological processes occurring in a portion of the hindbrain called the amygdala in order to uncover novel biochemical processes underlying REM sleep. A more comprehensive understanding of the complex biology of sleep will help further clarify the pathological processes that underlie narcolepsy and other sleep disorders.

Parasomnias

Parasomnia is a general term that encompasses a group of disorders that occur in semi-awake states. *Para* in this instance refers to "faulty" while *somnia* comes from the Latin word *somnus*, for *sleep*. Sometimes sleep specialists refer to parasomnias as disorders of partial arousal or disorders that interfere with the transitions between REM sleep and non-REM sleep—those twilight periods when one is not fully awake nor sound asleep.[46]

Typically, parasomnias are grouped into four categories, determined by when they occur in the sleep cycle: arousal disorders (sleepwalking, night terrors, and confusional arousals); sleep-wake transition disorders (sleep starts, sleep talking, and rhythmic movement disorders); REM sleep disorders (nightmares, REM sleep behavior disorder [RBD]); and other parasomnias (such as **enuresis** [bed-wetting]).

People who experience parasomnias usually do not remember them. Because a number of parasomnias, such as sleepwalking, commonly affect youngsters more often than adults, some are covered in more detail in Chapter 8: Sleep Disorders in Children.

AROUSAL DISORDERS

Disorders of arousal are common in children, but can also first appear in young adults and adults. Epidemiological studies show that arousal disorders occur in 10 percent of adults.

More recent research suggests there is a hereditary link with these disorders. In people who are predisposed to disorders of arousal, certain triggers have been identified, including sleep deprivation, drinking alcoholic beverages, and taking certain medications. EEG analyses in patients with disorders of arousal suggest an instability of slow-wave sleep, particularly during the first slow-wave sleep period of the night.[47]

Sleepwalking

There's an old myth that says if you wake a sleepwalker you will "scare him to death." In Carlos Schenck's book *Sleep: The Mysteries, the Problems, and the Solutions,* he says this sentiment comes from some primitive cultures in which it was thought that a sleepwalker's soul left his body during sleep, so if you roused the sleepwalker his soul would be lost for good.

Often, sleepwalking occurs without warning. A sleeper will rise, jump up, or even bolt from the bed and run. Some people act out what they are dreaming. They may move furniture, get dressed, even climb out a window. Sleepwalking may be accompanied by talking.

Typical sleepwalking signs include a glassy-eyed stare or blank expression. Sometimes sleepers can be heard talking but their words may sound jumbled and make no sense, especially in children. The sleeper may express bewilderment if he or she wakes up in a place other than his or her own bed. Amnesia upon waking may also occur.

Doctors say roommates and family members can guide a sleepwalker gently back to bed with an encouraging voice or gesture. If a sleepwalker looks like he may hurt himself by tripping, falling, or cutting himself, for example, try waking him up in a soothing, gentle fashion. Yelling at or shaking a sleepwalker awake may elicit physical aggression.[48]

Figure 7.1 Typical sleepwalking symptoms include a glassy-eyed stare or blank expression. © *Carol and Mike Werner/Phototake*

Sleepwalking is more common in children, but it can occur in adults, typically men. Adult sleepwalkers tend to be more physical and aggressive than children and have a higher incidence of injuries. Sleepwalking also appears to run in families.

Sleepwalking may occur several times a month and have no major impact on the sleeper or housemates, but if it persists regularly (a family member may witness nightly ramblings) and the sleepwalker is fatigued by day or sustains injuries from his nocturnal wanderings, a visit to a sleep specialist is recommended so that safety can be discussed. Placing a wind chime or bells in the doorway of a sleepwalker's room can help rouse him just enough to help him realize where he is and head back to bed.

Night Terrors

This disorder occurs when someone suddenly cries out and shows signs of fright during arousal from slow-wave sleep (non-REM) sleep. It is more common in children. Terrors are disconcerting because witnesses may think the sleeper is in pain or very frightened. Observers may even think the sleeper is awake and aware because people having night terrors sometimes sit up with their eyes open. A person experiencing a terror, however, is unresponsive when spoken to or touched. Awakening him in the middle of the terror may also be difficult, upsetting, or confusing to him. The sleeper usually cannot remember the experience the next morning. Pediatricians often recommend parents not to wake their child because the child will pass through the terror eventually and return to normal sleep behavior.

Confusional Arousals

More often seen in children, confusional arousals do affect some adults. Sometimes they're referred to as sleep drunkenness because a person may sit up in bed and feel overwhelmingly disoriented and confused. They do not usually get up out of bed like sleepwalkers, but may do odd things they don't remember later. Episodes may last anywhere from 5 to 45 minutes and normally happen within the first part of the night during arousal from deep sleep. Being over-tired has been linked to confusional arousals.

SLEEP-WAKE TRANSITION DISORDERS

Sleep-wake transition disorders include parasomnias that occur during the period when a person is transitioning between wakefulness and sleep, or when a sleeper is moving between sleep stages. Rhythmic movement disorder, sleep starts, sleep talking, and nocturnal leg cramps fall into this category.

Sleep Starts

Almost everyone knows the feeling of a sleep start; that falling sensation right before you nod off and the sudden jerk of your body in response. They are exactly what they feel like, brief contractions of muscles in the legs, arms, and sometimes head. Occasionally, in some people they can be very strong and frequent, causing insomnia. In such cases, an evaluation by a doctor or sleep specialist is advised.

Sleep Talking

Sleep talking is common in children. A child may chat, laugh, or cry out during sleep and typically won't remember it the next day. Stress, fever, sleep terrors, and even apnea may influence sleep talking, according to sleep expert William Dement in his book *The Promise of Sleep* (Delacorte Press, 1999). It usually bothers those who share a room with the sleeper more than the sleeper himself. There is usually no need to treat sleep talking.

Rhythmic Movement Disorder

Rhythmic movement disorder is sometimes referred to as head banging. Usually it appears in very young children, under the age of 12 months. It typically appears right before sleep. Like other parasomnias, it is very disconcerting. A child will repeatedly bang his or her head back against a pillow. Sometimes body rocking and rolling occur as well. Children typically outgrow it and there is usually no treatment other than parental reassurance.

REM SLEEP DISORDERS

REM sleep disorders strike the sleeper during REM sleep, or the period when sleepers are dreaming. They can be mild or occasionally extreme. In extreme cases, patients and family members should seek out help from their family doctor or a sleep specialist to learn coping strategies.

Nightmares

Nightmares are scary, vivid, and disturbing dreams that occur during REM sleep. They're more common in children and usually awaken the sleeper, who often will remember the upsetting content of the dream. They commonly happen in the later part of the night. Most children experience nightmares at one time or another. Three percent of preschool- and school-aged children experience frequent nightmares, according a 2004 Sleep in America poll by the National Sleep Foundation. Stress, a change in routine, or a difficult time in a child's life can precipitate nightmares. Soothing and reassuring a child will help reduce her post-nightmare emotions, and a nightlight, stuffed animal, or other security object can help. In a 2007 Swedish study, researchers found that sleep problems—especially insomnia and nightmares—are common among people who attempt suicide. In interviews with 165 adults who were admitted to medical units or psychiatric wards after attempting suicide, the researchers found that 89 percent reported having at least one sleep problem. The most common problem was trouble falling asleep, but 66 percent complained of nightmares as well. They found that nightmares were associated with a fivefold increase in risk for suicide, even after adjusting for psychiatric illness. In their conclusion, the scientists suggested that sleep problems be evaluated in patients with depression and mental illness.[49]

REM Sleep Behavior Disorder (RBD)

People with RBD act out their dreams. It happens when the normal paralysis that appears during REM sleep does not occur. Hitting, running, jumping, and kicking are typical. RBD can be

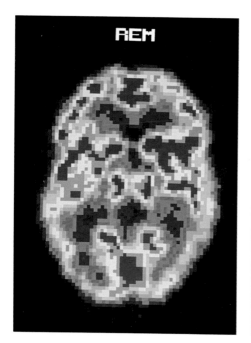 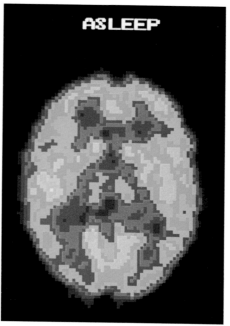

Figure 7.2 Colored Positron Emission Tomography (PET) scan of the brain during REM (rapid eye movement) sleep *(left)* and during NREM sleep *(right)*. Color-coding depicts active cerebral brain areas (red) and inactive areas (blue). During the REM sleep phase, the brain is active and dreaming, showing similar activity when awake. In the non-REM phase of sleep the brain is in a deeper, less active sleep. PET scanning shows metabolic activity of the brain. © *Hank Morgan/Photo Researchers, Inc.*

dangerous to the sleeper, but is also concerning for family members and roommates because it is associated with violent behavior. The prevalence of RBD is believed to be around 0.5 percent. Ninety percent of people with RBD are male, and most cases begin after age 50. The drug clonazepam is helpful in reducing symptoms in 90 percent of cases.[50] REM sleep behavior disorder occurs during REM sleep, and during REM sleep, the electrical activity of the brain recorded by an electroencephalogram looks similar to the electrical activity that occurs during wakeful periods. The brain's neurons function during REM sleep a lot like they do during waking periods, but during REM sleep normal sleepers experience temporary muscle paralysis. In REM sleep behavior disorder, the distinctions between the different states breaks down and the characteristics of one state carry over or into the others. Though it is unclear why it happens, sleep researchers think that perhaps neurological "barriers" that separate normal sleep states don't function correctly.[51]

At least half of RBD cases are related to recognized neurological conditions, including narcolepsy, Parkinson's disease, multiple system atrophy, and certain types of dementia. RBD may precede other features of these diseases by a decade. It is thought that some medications, such as selective serotonin reuptake inhibitors (SSRIs), may bring it on.[52]

Sleep Disorders in Children

It is not unusual for children to suffer from sleep troubles now and again—phases where falling asleep is difficult or when night wakings occur because of bad dreams or illness. New babies need time to establish routine sleep patterns in the first months after birth. Sometimes, however, a child may have a more serious sleep-related problem that requires medical help. Daytime sleepiness, chronic crankiness, difficulty focusing on schoolwork and home tasks, and chronic fatigue are a few of the hallmarks of a childhood sleep disorder. Many sleep experts believe children with sleep disorders often go undiagnosed because their conditions are overlooked or mistaken for other more common childhood illnesses and behaviors. The three most common childhood sleep disorders are obstructive sleep apnea (OSA); parasomnias, which include night terrors, sleepwalking and talking, and enuresis (bed-wetting); and narcolepsy.

SLEEP APNEA

Six-year-old Anton never seemed well rested. Even though his parents thought they were putting him to sleep early enough for him to get a good night's sleep, he always awoke in a grumpy mood and his teacher said she noticed Anton often yawned in class and was cranky and irritable with the other kindergarteners. His parents slowly adjusted Anton's bedtime from 8 p.m. each evening to 7 p.m., hoping the extra hour would help.

Anton woke at 7 each morning and was often getting more than the recommended amount of sleep for his age. The bedtime change, however, did not improve his school-day behavior.

In another family, four-year-old Kim's mom, Margaret, called her pediatrician one day full of anxiety. She reported that every night Kim slept, the child would stop breathing at times. Just as Margaret thought Kim would never take another breath and she was ready to shake her, Kim would snort and snore and resume breathing again. "It goes on all night. I've taken to sleeping in the same room with her, in case I need to wake her up to start breathing again. I am really worried," Margaret said.

Anton and Kim each have sleep apnea. While Anton's parents thought snoring was normal (which it is not) and Margaret became very worried by her daughter's nocturnal grunts and snores, both children's parents sensed that something was amiss while their child slept. Since a child is unaware of his nighttime habits—because he's asleep or never fully wakes during his brief wakings to resume breathing—a parent's efforts to help his or her child are pivotal.

Sleep Apnea Symptoms in Children

Obstructive sleep apnea and central sleep apnea are each found in children. The most common symptoms of obstructive sleep apnea include snoring, loud or noisy breathing, and mouth breathing; brief periods of no breathing, when air is not moving through the nose, mouth, and lungs, and which last for only seconds; restlessness during sleep, including frequent arousals or tossing and turning; sleeping in odd positions, sitting up or with neck arched backwards (hyperextended) in order to open the airway; behavior problems, such as irritability, crankiness, frustration, hyperactivity, and difficulty paying attention; and sleepiness during the day, yawning, and lack of energy. School problems may also be a symptom—a child may be mistakenly

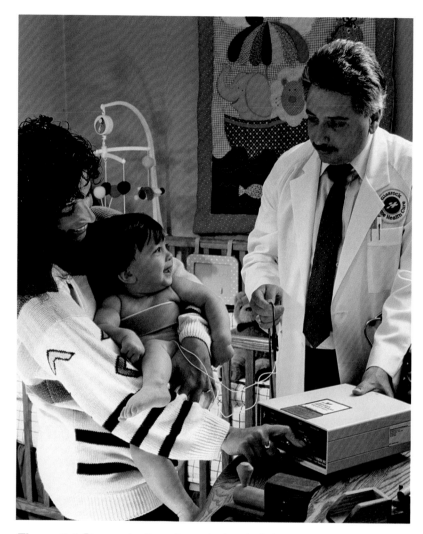

Figure 8.1 Demonstration of an electronic infant apnea monitoring system, showing an infant connected to the device via a cuff around the chest. © *Tim Hazael, The BOC Group plc/Photo Researchers, Inc.*

labeled "slow" or "lazy." Bed-wetting and frequent infections of the ear, nose, and throat may also be symptomatic. Symptoms may vary from child to child, however, and may resemble other conditions or medical problems.

Sleep apnea is always serious and can endanger a child's life, especially in infants who breathe more quickly and have a greater need for oxygen per minute. Periods of loud, noisy breathing in babies indicates the airway is partially or fully blocked. Other sleep apnea symptoms in babies may include pale, clammy skin, blue-tinged coloring around the mouth and fingernails, and seeming limp and unresponsive.

The immediate response to an apnea episode, if a sleeping child is struggling for breath or has ceased breathing and is not waking up to breathe on her own, is to gently shake or rouse the child so she begins breathing again. Parents or guardians should follow up by calling a pediatrician. The doctor may ask the parent and/or child to fill out a sleep questionnaire and may also refer the family to one or all of the following specialists: an otolaryngologist, also called an ENT, or ear, nose and throat physician; a pulmonary doctor; or a pediatric sleep medicine specialist. If sleep apnea is suspected, parents should be wary of medications that may depress breathing, such as painkillers, because they may exacerbate the apnea.

A specialist may refer the child for an overnight sleep study called a polysomnography (discussed below in more detail), and an evaluation of the upper-airway. X rays or other diagnostic tests may be required as well.

Treatment of Childhood Sleep Apnea

Once the cause of sleep apnea is uncovered, a treatment can be prescribed. Since enlarged tonsils and adenoids are the most common cause of obstructive sleep apnea in children, surgery to remove them, called a tonsillectomy and adenoidectomy, is usually recommended. An ear, nose, and throat specialist will be consulted if this is the case. Surgery is also sometimes needed if a child has sleep apnea because of a malformation of the craniofacial area. Birth defects and/or earlier trauma, because of a fall or car accident for example, may alter normal breathing ability.

It is also more common for overweight children to have sleep apnea. The extra fat tissue in the neck can interfere with breathing at night when a youngster is prone. If this is the root of a child's sleep apnea, weight loss and exercise may be prescribed and may have significant positive impact.

If surgery and other treatments are not effective, continuous positive airway pressure (CPAP) may be helpful. Many adults use CPAP for the same condition. A sleeping child wears a mask over the nose that is connected by a tube to a machine that gently blows air through the nasal passages and into the airway. The constant light air pressure keeps the airway open and allows the child to breathe normally during sleep.

It is important that a child with sleep apnea is treated or he could suffer irreversible problems. Over time, OSA can lead to poor growth, high blood pressure, and heart problems. It can impact learning and behavior as well. In all cases, the specific treatment for obstructive sleep apnea depends on many factors and is tailored for each child.

CHILDHOOD PARASOMNIAS

Pediatric parasomnias refer to a range of sleep disorders found in children. They are typically mild, but when disorders such as sleepwalking and night terrors become severe, disruptive or dangerous to the sleeper or his or her family, medical care is advised.

Sleepwalking and Sleep Talking

Every night, six-year-old Maria's parents would tuck her into bed snugly and say good night. One morning, Maria's mother, Rosa, went to her daughter's room to wake her up for school and Maria was missing. Alarmed, the family made a thorough search of the house, and her parents finally found the young-ster sleeping soundly on the couch in the family room. Maria said she had no recollection of how she got there. Every few weeks the same scenario would occur. Maria's pediatrician recommended she undergo a sleep center evaluation.

Sleep specialists confirmed that Maria is a sleepwalker. They recommended that her parents lock the doors and windows each night and make sure there are no objects on stairs or in hallways that could cause injury. They said medicine was not necessary unless Maria's nocturnal ambulations changed and put her at risk, for example, if she left the house or exhibited violent behavior toward herself or others while sleeping. The scientific term for sleepwalking is *somnambulism.* Sleep experts describe it as a series of complex behaviors that are initiated during slow-wave sleep and result in walking while still asleep. Though adults sleepwalk at times, it is more common in chil-dren. About 5 percent of children are prone to sleepwalking. Sleepwalking episodes usually occur in NREM (nonrapid eye movement) sleep, a period of slow-wave deep sleep character-ized by low brain activity. A sleepwalking child does not remem-ber his actions from the night before.

Somniloquy, or sleep talking, sometimes accompanies sleep-walking, and often sounds like incomprehensible mutterings. A parent may witness a child sitting up in bed, walking about the room, or the child running and screaming when he sleepwalks and talks. In some cases, a child may urinate in an inappropriate place, use obscene words he would not use when awake, or he may fall and injure himself.

Doctors are not sure why people sleepwalk or why children are more prone to it than adults. They do believe there may be a family link. Overtiredness, stress (because of parental discord, for example), fever, or medications may also play a role.

Sleepwalking and talking may appear once a month and be mild, but in some cases the events can occur more often and can be violent in nature. If a child demonstrates severe symptoms, nightly episodes involving physical injury, or if a sleepwalker leaves the house during an episode, the family should seek medical help immediately.

A child may feel embarrassed and anxious if he learns about his nocturnal behavior. Experts say it is important to handle his or her feelings with sensitivity or other sleep issues may arise. A child should be reassured that he will probably outgrow the behavior over time.[53]

Pavor Nocturnus: Night Terrors

The first time four-year-old Terrance woke up his parents with a blood-curdling scream, his mother thought he was in severe pain. A call to the pediatrician reassured her that he was probably experiencing a night terror. The doctor reassured her that Terrance will not remember the terrors in the morning and that they cause no lasting emotional impact. Talking to Terrance in a soothing tone sometimes seems to help, but his mother has learned not to wake him from the events because he will eventually go back to sleep on his own.

Though it is not clear why people and especially children have night terrors, scientists do know that night terrors often occur in the first half of the night during deep stage 3 and 4 non-REM sleep. Individuals generally do not remember night terrors. This contrasts with nightmares, which occur during REM sleep and which a person can remember.

During a night terror, a child may scream. He may sit up and appear wide-eyed, and clench or gnash his teeth. It is difficult to talk with a child who is having a night terror, but some parents believe that using a calming voice may help sooth their young one. A night terror may be quick or could last as long as 20 minutes.

Trying to wake a child can make the night terror worse, some experts say, although the reason is unknown. Night terrors have not generated the same research-focus as other parasomnias because they tend to go away and cause little harm, except perhaps anxiety for parents.

Night terrors are more common in boys than girls. Hallmarks of night terrors may include sudden awakening from sleep, persistent fear or terror that occurs at night, screaming, sweating, confusion, rapid heart rate, no recall of "bad dreams" or nightmares (unable to explain what happened but may have a sense of frightening images, or has no memory of the event when they awaken the next day), inability to fully wake up, and difficult to comfort.[54]

Parent education by pediatricians and sleep specialists can help parents cope with this upsetting parasomnia. If the night terrors are causing family distress, for example, a sibling who shares the same bedroom may awaken from the events, some doctors recommend scheduled awakenings for the afflicted child. So, for instance, if a child always has night terrors at 11 p.m., wake him at 10:30 for a minute and then let him go back to sleep. Often the night terror can be avoided this way.

Doctors often recommend more rest, as it appears overtired and overstressed children are more likely to experience this parasomnia than others. Comfort and reassurance usually eases the child out of his terror, but if symptoms persist, psychotherapy or counseling may be appropriate in some cases. On occasion, benzodiazepine medications (such as diazepam, known commonly by the commercial name Valium) are used at bedtime and will often reduce night terrors. However, medication is not often recommended to treat this disorder because most children don't usually remember the event and outgrow night terrors.

Sleep Enuresis: Bed-wetting

Susan, a single mother of two who worked the night shift at a newspaper office, often came home in the early morning to learn from the babysitter that her younger daughter, Janey, a preschooler, had wet the bed again. The family lived in a small apartment and many days Susan ended up in the building's basement washing sheets instead of getting much-needed rest. "One night, out of sheer exhaustion, I asked Janey to please try to wait until she woke up to use the bathroom. All of our sheets were dirty. I hadn't had time to wash the extra set that day," Susan says. Maybe it was the power of suggestion, but Janey never wet the bed again.

There is no medical evidence that shows Susan's approach works with all children, but she is certainly not alone in her efforts to help her young child overcome bed-wetting. Bed-wetting is a source of worry and frustration for parents, and sometimes embarrassment for children. It's not uncommon, affecting as many as 20 percent of children in the United States—or about 7 million— as well as some adolescents.

Most children will grow out of it by school age because it is usually tied to bladder control, which is a complex function impacted by nerves, muscles, the spinal cord, and brain. Some toddlers' bodies may not be physically mature enough to respond to signals yet that tell them to wake up and use the bathroom.

Children who are older than six, or who have not been bed-wetters but begin to have problems, could have an underlying problem and should be seen by a physician. Diabetes, constipation, urinary tract obstruction, and urinary tract infections may be to blame for the condition. Emotional issues may be at the root, too, including stress related to parents divorcing or a change in schools.

Adults should treat bed-wetting with patience. Parents should never yell at or shame a child. In most cases, he will grow out of it in time. Lifestyle changes that may help include reducing liquids in the evening, cutting out caffeinated beverages, and using diapers or absorbent pads to reduce cleanup.

NARCOLEPSY

Narcolepsy can happen in children and adults. It is a sleep disorder that causes uncontrollable sleepiness during the day. Scientists estimate that as many as 200,000 Americans have this sleep disorder, but that less than 25 percent of them are diagnosed. Only about 4 percent of narcoleptics are diagnosed before age 15.[55]

In recent years, there has been an increased awareness that narcolepsy can develop during childhood and may be linked to behavioral disorders, such as attention-deficit/hyperactivity disorder, depression, and sometimes psychosis. Scientists sponsored by the National Institute of Neurological Disorders and Stroke are conducting a large epidemiological study to understand the prevalence of narcolepsy in children ages 2 to 14 who have been diagnosed with attention-deficit/hyperactivity disorder.[56]

Symptoms

The symptoms of narcolepsy can appear all at once or may develop slowly over many years. The four most common symptoms are excessive daytime sleepiness, cataplexy, sleep paralysis, and hypnagogic hallucinations. Excessive daytime sleepiness is usually one of the first narcoleptic symptoms to crop up, and it may be the only apparent one for years. Narcoleptic children often feel tired or complain of tiredness more often than normal. They nod off at normal sleep-inducing events, such as dull classes, but will also fall asleep in the middle of conversations, or in more risky situations such as in a pool or while driving a car. It's not uncommon for parents and instructors to think the child is daydreaming or acting inattentive.

A child may experience cataplexy, a brief and sudden loss of muscle tone, while laughing or feeling some other strong emotion, such as anger, sadness, or surprise. They may collapse on the floor or their head may droop. Cataplexy episodes can last a few seconds or minutes. About 60 percent of children with narcolepsy experience cataplexy.

Sleep paralysis is the feeling one gets when falling asleep or just waking up, when the muscles are unable to move. It can be scary for a child because he may experience paralysis and hypnagogic hallucinations at the same time. Hypnagogic hallucinations are very vivid, dreamlike experiences that happen when a child is nodding off or waking up in the morning. For example, he may think he sees a monster in the room, yet cannot move away from it because his muscles are temporarily paralyzed. Touching someone experiencing sleep paralysis usually rouses him or her. Hypnagogic hallucinations occur in 40 percent to 60 percent of narcoleptics. According to the National Institute of Neurological Disorders and Stroke, 50 percent to 70 percent of adults with narcolepsy experience hypnagogic hallucinations. Some children and teens who are not narcoleptic also experience them.

Cause of Narcolepsy
The exact cause of narcolepsy is unknown. Studies using gene markers show that the disorder may be genetic. Scientists have also found that those with narcolepsy may have fewer neuron that produce hypocretin, a hormone linked to wakefulness.[57] The disorder may be aggravated by conditions that cause insomnia, such as disruption of work schedules. Narcolepsy episodes usually occur after meals, but any nonstimulating situation, or being in situations where there is little movement, can exacerbate it.

Narcolepsy appears to run in families. One percent of children with the disorder have a narcoleptic parent, 40 times that of the overall population. It is thought that 8 percent to 12 percent of people diagnosed with narcolepsy have a close family member, like a sibling or parent, with the disorder. Forty percent of narcoleptics have a family member with a medical history marked by excessive daytime sleepiness.

It's interesting to note, however, that as with other medical conditions, genetics may not be a sole player in getting the disorder. In studies of identical twins, there have been cases where one had narcolepsy and one did not, suggesting other factors may be at play, such as environment and infection.[58]

Treatment for Young Narcoleptics

After a polysomnogram (PSG) and a multiple sleep latency test (MSLT) have been performed, doctors can rule out other sleep disorders such as sleep apnea, and help parents manage their child's narcolepsy. If REM sleep is noted during the sleep latency test, narcolepsy is very likely. It may take several night studies to confirm the diagnosis.

There is no cure for narcolepsy, but it can be controlled so that a child can lead a normal life. Treatment can be tailored to a child's specific needs with a mix of medication, behavioral counseling, and managing environment.

Though it might be tempting to keep a child awake with over-the-counter products and caffeinated beverages, such as colas and chocolate, trying to medicate that way is not recommended and can actually be dangerous. A child's doctor can prescribe drugs that may help control excessive daytime sleepiness, cataplexy, and disrupted sleep. If a medication causes unwanted side effects, parents can work with the doctor to adjust it until a balance of minimal side effects but control of symptoms can be achieved.

Behavioral modification therapy, which involves making lifestyle changes, can help a narcoleptic child reduce problems as well. Parents can employ a strict sleep-wake schedule for their child, putting him to bed and waking him up at the same time every day. Short naps a couple of times a day can be scheduled as well, and may be effective in reducing daytime tiredness. Regular physical activity is also recommended.

Because dull, repetitive tasks can bring on a narcoleptic event, parents and teachers may wish to keep a narcoleptic child's schedule interesting and active, avoiding any activities that might be dangerous such as driving, swimming, or cooking, except when a child can be monitored or they know the child will be alert.

Understanding narcolepsy can be a family's secret weapon in beating its symptoms. If parents, teachers, and acquaintances do not understand the disorder, a child's health and happiness may be risked. Daytime fatigue may be mistaken for laziness, boredom, or lack of ability, and the reprimands a child receives may be detrimental. The experiences of cataplexy and dreaming during wakefulness may be wrongly seen as a psychiatric problem. Educated family members and friends can help support the young person. Most importantly, teachers should understand the disorder. Small adjustments in the classroom can make a tremendous difference with regard to a student's self-esteem and ability to obtain a good education.

SLEEP STUDIES CAN ILLUMINATE PROBLEMS IN CHILDREN

Disrupted rest can be detrimental to a child's life, interfering with his or her ability to concentrate and learn at school, and leading to social and behavioral problems with family, teachers, and other children. If parents or pediatricians suspect a sleep disorder may be disrupting a child's nighttime rest, a sleep study may be recommended, including a polysomnogram and a multiple sleep latency test. A PSG must be conducted at night during a child's normal sleep hours. The MSLT is performed by

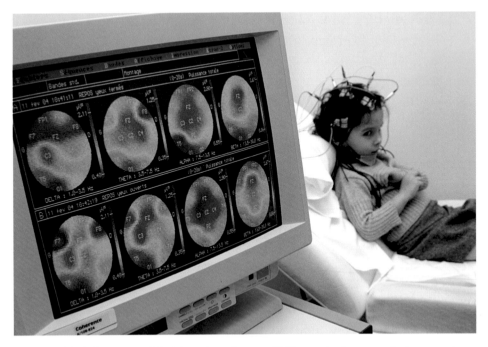

Figure 8.2 A four-year-old girl undergoing an EEG, or electroencephalogram, to monitor the electrical activity of her brain. EEGs can help specialists identify sleep disorders in children. © AJPhoto/Photo Researchers, Inc.

day and measures a person's tendency to fall asleep. It can help doctors see whether isolated REM sleep occurs at unexpected times of day, which would indicate a disorder.

There are not many sleep clinics that specialize in pediatric problems, but most of the sleep labs in the United States are able to accommodate and evaluate children as well as adults. Pediatricians, pediatric sleep specialists, and others, such as pediatric pulmonary and neurology experts, often will weigh in on sleep test results and suggest treatments appropriate for a child.

Many sleep centers provide a bed for a child's parent or guardian, and the child or teen can bring along a favorite stuffed animal, blanket, or something from home that helps him or her feel more at ease. Lights are kept low and the room quiet and calm.

Before the nighttime study begins, a sleep technologist will place electrodes on the child's body to monitor his or her quality and quantity of sleep. While the child sleeps, the sensors track breathing, blood pressure, muscle movements, heart rate, and oxygen intake to help determine whether the child's sleep problem is caused by breathing trouble, a movement disorder, or an issue related to maintaining sleep. Sensors on

A Word About SIDS

Sudden infant death syndrome (SIDS), also sometimes called crib death, is a fatal and unexplained syndrome that affects seemingly healthy babies, usually between 1 and 12 months of age. It occurs at night because of the cessation of breathing.

Researchers believe risk factors may include low birth weight, infection, bottle-feeding; smoking, drug addiction, or anemia in the mother, and poor socioeconomic background. Some experts think SIDS may be related to abnormalities in breathing and heart rate, possibly because of a fault in the brain stem.

Good obstetric and pediatric care, breastfeeding, and close observation of the baby are believed to help prevent SIDS. Experts continue to debate about the best sleep position to avoid SIDS, but most say keeping an infant off his belly and on his back or side is the safest sleep position. Some parents use alarm devices that detect when a baby stops breathing.[59]

the head allow an EEG to continually assess the child's stages of sleep.

Once the sleep study is completed, experts can use the information to diagnose and help manage possible conditions such as:

- Behavioral problems (bedtime struggles, night wakings)
- Parasomnias (sleepwalking, sleep terrors)
- Narcolepsy
- Circadian rhythm disorders (delayed sleep phase syndrome)
- Movement disorders (periodic limb movement disorder, head banging)
- Sleep apnea
- Chronic lung diseases
- Degenerative muscle disease with chronic respiratory failure
- Hypoventilation syndrome
- Respiratory control disorders

After sleep experts have evaluated the data, doctors may recommend such treatments as behavioral modification therapy, ventilatory support during sleep, medication, or surgery, depending on the diagnosis.

The Future
of Sleep Medicine

Only six decades ago, dream analysis was the most exciting thing happening in the scientific world of sleep. Much has changed in the ensuing years. Now, every year, thousands of scientists from around the globe gather for sleep medicine–related conferences, conduct research, and counsel and treat patients suffering from a vast number of sleep-related disorders. In addition, what was once a field of medicine primarily of interest to psychiatrists and psychologists has now drawn the attention of neurologists, pulmonary and cardiac experts, pediatricians, sports medicine doctors, allergists, and immunologists, among other medical specialists.

The year 2007 was a milestone year for the field of sleep medicine. For the first time, the field was officially recognized as a medical specialty—like the fields of dermatology and cardiology, for example—by the American Board of Medical Specialists. "That recognition has validated the clinical and scientific growth, the acceptance of the field, and the maturing of it," says physician Ronald Kramer, M.D., a spokesman for the American Academy of Sleep Medicine who treats patients at the Colorado Sleep Disorders Center in Denver.[60]

Despite the increased popularity and attention, many questions remain unanswered about the physical and emotional aspects and the impact sleep has on human beings. Sleep specialists say they have only just begun to chip away at finding treatments for many sleep disorders, such as narcolepsy and night terrors.

Kramer says the public health and societal issues regarding sleep are significant and therapists are ready to tackle them. He and other experts say there is a need for more public education about the health risks of sleep deprivation, which has been linked to increased disease, higher numbers of accidents, and reduced school and job performance. Problems such as insomnia, and whether to treat patients with behavioral or pharmaceutical solutions, also continue to be debated.

While some researchers are focusing on specific disorders and treatments, others remain committed to promoting messages that will help people achieve better-quality sleep and reduce sleep deprivation, a national epidemic, according to sleep experts Ronald Kramer and Jodi Mindell (associate director of The Sleep Center at The Children's Hospital of Philadelphia). "I think the real future of sleep medicine is about optimizing sleep to optimize health. Sleep is finally getting the attention it deserves next to diet and exercise, and people are learning that you can't fool Mother Nature. You can't get away with four hours of sleep and say you're doing fine," Kramer says.

Little by little, sleep researchers are unraveling details about the mysterious one-third of life humans spend asleep. Scientists in the field anticipate the next decade or two to usher in breakthroughs in the understanding of many sleep disorders, such as narcolepsy and insomnia. Geneticists hope to pinpoint the genes responsible for many inherited sleep disorders. Once a set of genes or gene products is identified that is involved in the regulation of sleep cycles, perhaps more targeted drug therapies can be developed to improve treatments for a range of sleep disorders. Other types of medications are being tested and used that may help shift workers, frequent travelers who suffer from

Two Little Peptides that May Reveal a Big Story

Recently, the discoveries of two related neuropeptide hormones have helped scientists better understand narcolepsy, a sleep disorder that causes severe sleepiness during the day. The peptides are referred to as orexin-A and B, or hypocretin 1 and 2. Whether they will ultimately be called orexins or hypocretins is still up for debate. Research indicates that the peptides, produced by a small group of cells in the hypothalamus, play an important biological role in wakefulness, and possibly food intake. Hypocretin 1 may be more biologically important than the second peptide, but more research is needed.[61]

Based on a number of early studies, scientists believe that orexin/hypocretin is involved in metabolic, circadian, and sleep/wake activity. Some research indicates that people and animals with hypocretin-deficiency suffer from narcolepsy. Hypocretin-based drugs could potentially treat narcoleptics with fewer side effects than the current crop of amphetamines.[62]

A study published in the May 25, 2005, issue of the *Journal of Neuroscience*, by Dr. Evelyn Lambe and colleagues at Yale University School of Medicine, suggested that hypocretin plays a role in attention and suggested that hypocretin and nicotine both may influence attention and performance. In the study, 10 adult rats were trained to pay attention to a stimulus, then choose a target to receive a food reward. After learning the task, the prefrontal cortices of the rats were infused with either saline, nicotine, a low dose of hypocretin, or a high dose of hypocretin. The results showed that doses of either nicotine or hypocretin improved the rats' ability to pay attention and perform the task. The rats that received higher doses of hypocretin or nicotine demonstrated improved accuracy under demanding conditions.[63]

jet lag, military personnel, and others who must cope with irregular sleep hours on a regular basis.[64]

Pediatric sleep experts say sleep apnea in children is also beginning to draw more interest on the research front, and they hope in the near future to better understand its underlying cause or causes and develop better treatments so that children will not suffer the serious effects sleep loss can have on learning and behavior. Pediatric sleep specialists are also learning how sleep deprivation and sleep disorders in children may affect behavior. It is thought that if some sleep problems are resolved in certain children with diagnoses such as hyperactivity, their school performance, emotional, and social difficulties may improve.[65]

Bruce Bender, a psychologist at National Jewish Medical and Research Center in Denver, Colorado, where he heads the division of pediatric behavioral health, says that sleep technology will continue to allow scientists in the field to make new and important discoveries. Newer devices, especially those that can monitor sleep at home, will uncover important details about the sleep habits of many patients. Devices such as the aptigraph, basically an especially sensitive motion detector, can be worn on the wrist while sleeping at home and will help measure sleep efficiency, or how much time in bed is actually spent sleeping. Brain imaging and new and improved sleep-monitoring devices will also help medical experts gain a better understanding of the brain's inner workings, which will benefit all fields of medicine.[66]

Kramer sends a mild warning to patients with sleep troubles, though. He notes that there are a plethora of questionable products being hawked, such as beds, light sensors, and so-called natural remedies, that have not been tested. He says to be wary of unqualified people who call themselves sleep experts, even some doctors, pushing what they believe will solve sleep problems. "Keep an eye out for frauds. The field of sleep medicine is prone to charlatanism," Kramer cautions.

Sleep is an active and dynamic state that greatly influences our waking hours. As sleep research attracts more interest and funding, scientists should unravel more of its mysteries. And gaining a thorough understanding of sleep's effect on our lives, and obtaining adequate sleep, will result in a healthier, happier society as a whole.

NOTES

1. U.S. Department of Health and Human Services, National Institutes of Health: National Heart, Lung, and Blood Institute, *Your Guide to Healthy Sleep* (NIH Publication No. 06-5271, November 2005), http://www.nhlbi.nih.gov/health/public/sleep/healthy_sleep.pdf (accessed May 29, 2008).

2. *Report of the Presidential Commission on the Space Shuttle Challenger Accident. Vol. 2, Appendix G. Human Factors Analysis.* Washington, DC: Government Printing Office; 1986.

3. Michael Twery (director of the National Center on Sleep Disorders Research Branch at the National Heart, Lung, and Blood Institute), interview by the author, October 11, 2007.

4. U.S. Department of Health and Human Services, *Your Guide to Healthy Sleep.*

5. U.S. Department of Health and Human Services, *Your Guide to Healthy Sleep.*

6. U.S. Nuclear Regulatory Commission, "Fact Sheet on the Three Mile Island Accident," http://www.nrc.gov/reading-rm/doc-collections/fact-sheets/3mile-isle.html (accessed May 21, 2008).

7. Ibid.

8. U.S. Department of Health and Human Services, *Your Guide to Healthy Sleep.*

9. U.S. Department of Health and Human Services, *Your Guide to Healthy Sleep.*

10. U.S. Department of Health and Human Services, *Your Guide to Health Sleep.*

11. Richard Castriotta (Memorial Hermann Hospital Sleep Disorders Center, Houson, Tex.), in discussion with author, November 30, 2007.

12. James E. Gangwisch et. al, "Short Sleep Duration as a Risk Factor for Hypertension: Analyses of the First National Health and Nutrition Examination Survey," *Hypertension* 47 (2006): 833-839; and U.S. Department of Health and Human Services, *Your Guide to Healthy Sleep.*

13. D. Kripke, "Mortality Associated with Sleep Duration and Insomnia." *Archives of General Psychiatry* 59 (2002): 131–136.

14. U.S. Department of Health and Human Services, *Your Guide to Healthy Sleep.*

15. National Institutes of Health, "Nine Hours of Sleep Key to 'Back to School' Success," news release, September 19, 2002, http://www.nhlbi.nih.gov/new/press/02-09-19.htm (accessed May 22, 2008).

16. William C. Dement and Christopher Vaughan, *The Promise of Sleep* (New York: Delacorte Press, 1999).

17. U.S. Department of Health and Human Services, *Your Guide to Healthy Sleep.*

18. H.P. Van Dongen, G. Maislin, J.M. Mullington, and D.F. Dinges, "The Cumulative Cost of Additional Wakefulness: Dose-Response Effects on Neurobehavioral Functions and Sleep Physiology from Chronic Sleep Restriction and Total Sleep Deprivation," *Sleep* 26 (2003): 117–126.

19. B. Adams and B. Williams, "Mother Won't Be Charged in Baby's Death:

The Sleep-Deprived Woman Forgot and Left her Daughter in a Car for more than Eight Hours." *Wisconsin State Journal*, October 10, 2003.

20. S. Campbell, "Effects of a Nap on Nighttime Sleep and Waking Function in Older Subjects," *Journal of the American Geriatrics Society* 53, no. 1 (2005): 48–53.

21. Craig Lambert, "Deep into Sleep: While Researchers Probe Sleep's Functions, Sleep Itself Is Becoming a Lost Art," *Harvard Magazine*, July–August 2005, http://harvardmagazine. com/2005/07/deep-into-sleep.html (accessed May 22, 2008).

22. M. Irwin, "Sleep Deprivation and Activation of Morning Levels of Cellular and Genomic Markers of Inflammation," *Archives of Internal Medicines* 166 (2006): 1756–1762.

23. U.S. Department of Health and Human Services, *Your Guide to Healthy Sleep.*

24. N. Ayas, D. White, J. Manson, M. Stampfer, F. Speizer, A. Malhotra, and F. Hu, "A Prospective Study of Sleep Duration and Coronary Heart Disease in Women," *Archives of Internal Medicine* 163 (2003): 205–209.

25. National Institute of Neurological Disorders and Stroke. "Brain Basics: Understanding Sleep," http://www. ninds.nih.gov/disorders/brain_basics/ understanding_sleep.htm#sleep_and_ disease (accessed May 22, 2008).

26. Gangwisch et. al, "Short Sleep Duration as a Risk Factor for Hypertension: Analyses of the First National Health and Nutrition Examination Survey."

27. The American Physiological Society, "Expecting an Afternoon Nap Can Reduce Blood Pressure," news release, October 15, 2007, http://www. the-aps.org/press/journal/07/55.htm (accessed May 22. 2008).

28. National Heart, Lung, and Blood Insitute, "What Causes Overweight and Obesity?" National Heart Lung and Blood Institute: Diseases and Conditions Index, http://www.nhlbi. nih.gov/health/dci/Diseases/obe/obe_ causes.html (accessed May 28, 2008).

29. K. Spiegel, "Sleep Curtailment in Healthy Young Men Is Associated with Decreased Leptin Levels, Elevated Ghrelin Levels, and Increased Hunger and Appetite," *Annals of Internal Medicine* 141, no. 11 (2004): 846–850.

30. American Academy of Sleep Medicine, "Insomnia," SleepEducation.com from the American Academy of Sleep Medicine, http://www.sleepeducation. com/Disorder.aspx?id=6 (accessed May 28, 2008).

31. S. Beaulieu-Bonneau, "Family History of Insomnia in a Population-Based Sample," *Sleep* 30, no. 12 (2007): 1739-1745.

32. Simon Beaulieu-Bonneau (École de Psychologie, Université Laval in Quebec, Canada), in discussion with the author, December 6, 2007.

33. Matthew R. Ebben, Ph.D. (assistant professor of psychology in neurology at Weill Medical College of Cornell University, New York, N.Y.), in discussion with the author, December 6, 2007.

34. Simon Beaulieu-Bonneau, in discussion with the author, December 6, 2007.

35. Associated Professional Sleep Societies, "Brief Use of Bright Light Therapy at Night Improves Sleep for People with Early-Morning Awakening Insomnia," news release, May 1, 2005, http://www.sleepeducation.com/Article.aspx?id=49 (accessed May 29, 2008).

36. Phil Gehrman (clinical associate professor of medicine and psychiatry at University of Pennsylvania Medical School), in discussion with the author, May 29, 2007.

37. Liz Johns (apnea patient), in discussion with author, December 6, 2007.

38. Ibid.

39. Ibid.

40. National Institute of Neurological Disorders and Stroke, "Brain Basics: Understanding Sleep," http://www.ninds.nih.gov/disorders/brain_basics/understanding_sleep.htm#sleep_disorders (accessed May 29, 2008).

41. National Center on Sleep Disorders Research, "Restless Legs Syndrome/Periodic Limb Movement Disorder," National Heart, Lung, and Blood Institute, http://www.nhlbi.nih.gov/health/prof/sleep/res_plan/section5/section5d.html (accessed May 29, 2008).

42. National Center on Sleep Disorders Research, "Restless Legs Syndrome/Periodic Limb Movement Disorder."

43. S. Litkin, Mayo Clinic Family Health Book, 3d ed. (New York: Harper Collins, 2003): 1264.

44. Stanford University School of Medicine, Center for Narcolepsy, "Center for Narcolepsy," http://med.stanford.edu/school/Psychiatry/narcolepsy (accessed May 30).

45. National Institute of Neurological Disorders and Stroke, "Narcolepsy Fact Sheet," http://www.ninds.nih.gov/disorders/narcolepsy/detail_narcolepsy.htm (accessed July 23, 2008).

46. National Center on Sleep Disorders Research, "National Sleep Disorders Research Plan," National Center on Sleep Disorders Research and National Heart, Lung, and Blood Institute-National Institutes of Health Web site, http://www.nhlbi.nih.gov/health/prof/sleep/res_plan/section5/section5f.html (accessed May 30, 2008).

47. Ibid.

48. C. Schenck, Sleep: The Mysteries, the Problems, and the Solutions (New York: Avery, 2007).

49. N. Sjöström, M. Waern, and J. Hetta, "Nightmares and Sleep Disturbances in Relation to Suicidality in Suicide Attempters." Sleep 30(1) (2007): 91–95.

50. National Center on Sleep Disorders Research, "National Sleep Disorders Research Plan."

51. National Sleep Foundation, "REM Behavior Disorder: When Your Dreams Become Real," http://www.sleepfoundation.org/site/c.huIXKjM0IxF/b.2464313/apps/nl/content3.asp?content_id=%7B78D5A886-6E44-44D7-8523-DEB1EE22BBED%7D&notoc=1 (accessed May 30, 2008).

52. National Center on Sleep Disorders Research, "National Sleep Disorders Research Plan."

53. Jodi A. Mindell, Ph.D. (associate director of the Sleep Center at The Children's Hospital of Philadelphia, and professor of psychology at Saint Joseph's University, Philadelphia), in discussion with the author, January 29, 2008.

54. Medline Plus, "Night Terrors," National Library of Medicine, http://www.nlm.nih.gov/medlineplus/ency/article/000809.htm (accessed May 30, 2008).

55. Judy A. Owens and Jodi A. Mindell, *Take Charge of Your Child's Sleep* (New York: Marlowe and Co., 2005).

56. National Institute of Neurological Disorders and Stroke, "Narcolepsy Fact Sheet."

57. Ibid.

58. American Academy of Sleep Medicine, "Scientists Believe They Have Found the Cause of Narcolepsy in the Human Brain," news release, August 29, 2000, http://www.sleepeducation.com/Article.aspx?id=16 (accessed July 21, 2008); R. Hayduk et al., "Monozygotic Twins with Narcolepsy: Preliminary Report," *Sleep Research* 25 (1996): 252.

59. Charles B. Clayman, ed., *The American Medical Association Encyclopedia of Medicine* (New York: Random House, 1989).

60. Ronald Kramer, M.D., (Colorado Sleep Disorders Center in Englewood, Colo.) in discussion with author, March 13, 2008.

61. Ronald Kramer, M.D., in discussion with author, March 13, 2008.

62. Alexis Madriga, "Snorting a Brain Chemical Could Replace Sleep," *Wired*, December 28, 2007, http://www.wired.com/science/discoveries/news/2007/12/sleep_deprivation (accessed February 5, 2008); S.A. Deadwyler, L. Porrino, J.M. Siegel, and R.E. Hampson, "Systemic and Nasal Delivery of Orexin-A (Hypocretin-1) Reduces the Effects of Sleep Deprivation on Cognitive Performance in Nonhuman Primates," *Journal of Neuroscience* 27, no. 52: 14239–14247.

63. National Institue on Drug Abuse. "Study Suggests that Hypocretin Plays a Role in Attention," February 1, 2006, American Academy of Sleep Medicine Web site, http://sleepeducation.com/Article.aspx?id=188 (accessed May 30, 2008).

64. Ronald Kramer, interview with author, March 13, 2008.

65. Jodi A. Mindell, Ph.D. (author of *Take Charge of Your Child's Sleep: The All in One Resource for Solving Sleep Problems in Kids and Teens*, and associate director of the Sleep Center at The Children's Hospital of Philadelphia, and professor of psychology at Saint Joseph's University, in Philadelphia), in discussion with the author, January 29, 3008.

66. Bruce Bender, M.D. (psychologist and head of the division of pediatric behavioral health, National Jewish Medical and Research Center in Denver, Colo.), in discussion with the author, March 18, 2008.

adenosine—A neurotransmitter associated with sleepiness.

Americans with Disabilities Act—Legislation that took effect July 26, 1992, and prohibits private employers, state and local governments, employment agencies, and labor unions from discriminating against qualified individuals with disabilities in job application procedures, hiring, firing, advancement, compensation, job training, and other terms, conditions, and privileges of employment.

amphetamines—A group of stimulant drugs.

anemia—A condition in which the person has less than the normal number of oxygen-carrying red blood cells. Patients with anemia may feel tired, appear pale, and fatigue easily.

anticonvulsants—Also known as anti-seizure medications. Developed primarily to reduce or control epileptic seizures, these drugs seem to work by slowing or blocking pain signals from damaged nerves.

barbiturates—A class of drugs used to treat insomnia prior to the 1960s, until the introduction of benzodiazepines.

benzodiazepines—A class of drugs used to treat insomnia, including medications such as Valium and Librium. They are also sometimes called benzodiazepine receptor agonists (BZRAs). Xanax and Restoril are often prescribed currently because they are more short-acting than earlier forms.

bruxism—Teeth grinding.

caffeine—An alkaloid stimulant found naturally in coffee. Caffeine is often added to other beverages.

cataplexy—Periods of muscle paralysis sometimes experienced by narcoleptics.

central nervous system (CNS)—The portion of the nervous system that includes the brain and spinal cord.

central sleep apnea—Also called primary sleep apnea. A breathing disorder characterized by brief interruptions in breathing during sleep. Occurs when the brain fails to send signals to the muscles that initiate respiration.

circadian rhythm—Any biological pattern based on a 24-hour cycle.

cognitive-behavioral therapy (CBT)—A system of therapy that focuses on unlearning/changing unhealthy behaviors and habits. For example, patients with insomnia who drink a lot of coffee are often advised by CBT experts to cut out caffeine since it is a stimulant.

continuous positive airway pressure (CPAP)—Commonly used by sleep apnea patients, a continuous positive airway pressure machine is often referred to as a CPAP. A fitted mask is placed over the nose of the patient to help deliver oxygen and keep the airways open during sleep.

CT scan—Computerized tomography scan, an X-ray technique that produces images of the body that visualize internal structures in cross section.

dopamine—A chemical messenger responsible for transmitting signals between one area of the brain, the substantia nigra, and the next relay station of the brain, the corpus striatum, to produce smooth, purposeful muscle activity.

dopamine agonist—Chemical compounds that mimic the action of the neurotransmitter dopamine

EEG—*See* electroencephalogram.

electroencephalogram (EEG)—The record of brain wave activity taken by an electroencephalograph. Tiny electrodes are temporarily attached to the head to measure the electrical impulses of the brain (also known as brain waves). Commonly used by sleep experts in sleep laboratories to help diagnose sleep disorders.

electroencephalograph—A device used to record brain wave activity.

electromyography—A test used to analyze electrical activity in muscle.

enuresis—Bed-wetting.

excessive daytime sleepiness (EDS)—A common symptom of narcolepsy, EDS is usually the first to become clinically apparent. It interferes with normal activities on a daily basis, regardless of whether patients have sufficient sleep at night. People with EDS describe it as a persistent sense of mental cloudiness, fatigue, a lack of energy, a depressed mood, or extreme exhaustion. Concentration at school and work is often poor, memory lapses may occur, and many find it is difficult to stay alert in passive situations.

ghrelin—Hormone that triggers hunger.

hypertension—Chronic condition of elevated blood pressure.

hypnagogic—Relating to the period of drowsiness preceding sleep.

hypocretin—Hormone believed to be linked to wakefulness and food intake. Also known as *orexin*.

hypothalamus—A tiny yet very important structure at the base of the brain that regulates sleep and wakefulness, as well as heart rate, appetite, blood sugar, temperature, and the release of hormones.

idiopathic—Arising from unknown cause.

insomnia—From the Latin words *no* and *somnus*, the term literally means *no sleep*. It is a disorder characterized by difficulty falling asleep, staying asleep, or waking up too early.

leptin—Hormone that helps to curb appetite.

melatonin—A hormone produced by the pineal gland, involved in regulating the sleep/wake cycle.

mixed sleep apnea—A combination of both obstructive sleep apnea and central sleep apnea.

multiple sleep latency test—A diagnostic tool often employed to test for narcolepsy.

MRI—Magnetic resonance imaging. A noninvasive way of taking pictures of the body using powerful magnets and radio waves.

narcolepsy—Characterized by extreme daytime sleepiness, and sometimes episodes of muscle paralysis (cataplexy), and hypnagogic hallucinations.

neurological disorder—Disorder of the nervous system.

neuron—A brain cell that can transmit information.

neuropathy—Disease or malfunction of the nerves.

neurotransmitter—A chemical in the brain that carries nerve impulses from one neuron to the next.

night terror—A sudden awakening from sleep in which the sleeper may show extreme fear, scream, sit up, or move about. Most common in children.

nocturnal leg cramps—Involuntary muscle contractions in the calves, soles, and feet during the night.

non-REM sleep—Sometimes called NREM sleep, nonrapid eye movement sleep is characterized by dreamlessness. On an electroencephalogram, brain waves usually appear slow and of high voltage. Breathing and heart rate are slow as well.

obstructive sleep apnea—A breathing disorder characterized by brief interruptions in breathing during sleep. Occurs when air is unable to flow in and out of the nose or mouth because of a structural problem in the airway, such as enlarged tonsils.

opiates—Medications and illegal drugs derived from the poppy plant, although some opiates are synthetically made. Opiates are narcotic sedatives that depress the central nervous system, reduce pain, and cause sleepiness.

pallidotomy—A surgical procedure that destroys a small area of brain cells using a tiny electrical probe.

parasomnia—Characterized by undesirable physical and/or verbal behaviors, parasomnias are disruptive sleep-related disorders that can occur during arousals from REM sleep or partial arousals from NREM sleep.

periodic limb movement disorder (PLMD)—Disorder characterized by repetitive, stereotyped movements of the limbs, often the legs, during sleep. Involves flexing of the big toe, ankle, knee, and hip, but in some people the upper extremities are involved.

pineal gland—A pea-size structure close to the center of the brain that secretes melatonin.

polysomnogram (PSG)—Recordings used in sleep studies, including the electroencephalogram, electrooculograph (which measures eye movement), the electromyography (which measures muscle movement), and the electrocardiograph (which measures heart activity).

pulmonary—Related to the lung.

REM sleep behavior disorder—In normal rapid-eye-movement (REM) sleep, the body is motionless, and the muscles immobilized. In patients with REM sleep behavior disorder, however, muscles are active and the patient may act out dreams.

REM sleep—Sleep during which rapid eye movement occurs. On an encephalographic brain recording, REM sleep is characterized by rapid, low-voltage brain waves.

restless legs syndrome (RLS)—A physiological condition characterized by a creeping, tingly feeling in the legs, which may cause sleep disruption.

rhythmic movement disorder—A group of repeated movements (usually in the head and neck) which occur right before sleep, typically seen in children.

selective serotonin reuptake inhibitors (SSRIs)—A group of antidepressants that block the reabsorption of the neurotransmitter serotonin in the brain.

sleep apnea—Temporary cessation of breathing during sleep, episodes of which may last from 10 to 60 seconds at a time. Snoring often accompanies sleep apnea.

sleep cycle—The progress of sleep ranging from NREM (including all four stages) through REM sleep.

sleep debt—The accumulated result of not getting enough sleep.

sleep disorders—Any problem that affects, disrupts, or involves sleep. Common sleep disorders include sleep apnea, restless legs syndrome, and insomnia.

sleep hygiene—A collection of habits that help lead to healthy sleep, including avoiding caffeine, alcohol, and rigorous activity before bedtime, as well as maintaining healthy lifestyle choices such as good nutrition and regular exercise, and a normal sleep schedule.

sleep lab—A place where sleep experts test and diagnose patients with suspected sleep problems. Many major medical centers affiliated with medical universities have a sleep laboratory.

sleep starts—Also called hypnic or hypnagogic jerks. Sudden, brief, strong contractions of the body that can occur as a person falls asleep.

somnolence—Sleepiness or drowsiness.

tricyclic antidepressants (TCAs)—Class of antidepressant drugs first used in the 1960s. Named for the drugs' chemical structure, they block the reabsorption of neurotransmitters serotonin and norepinephrine, and dopamine to a lesser extent.

valerian—A sedative made from the dried roots of the valerian plant.

Books

Dement, William C., and Chris Vaughan. *The Promise of Sleep.* New York: Dellacorte Books, 1999.

Epstein, Lawrence, and Steven Mardon. *The Harvard Medical School Guide to a Good Night's Sleep.* New York: McGraw-Hill, 2006.

Jacobs, Gregg, and Herbert Benson. *Say Good Night to Insomnia: The Six-Week, Drug-Free Program Developed at Harvard Medical School.* New York: Holt Paperbacks, 1999.

Lombardo, Gerard T. *Sleep to Save Your Life: The Complete Guide to Living Longer and Healthier Through Restorative Sleep.* New York: Collins, 2005.

Walsleben, Joyce A., and Rita Baron-Faust. *A Woman's Guide to Sleep.* New York: Three Rivers Press, 2000.

Web Sites

American Counseling Association
http://www.counseling.org

DrowsyDriving.org
http://www.drowsydriving.org

The Mayo Clinic: Sleep
http://www.mayoclinic.com/health/sleep/SL99999

National Center on Sleep Disorders Research
http://www.nhlbi.nih.gov/about/ncsdr

National Heart, Lung, and Blood Institute: Sleep Disorders Information
http://www.nhlbi.nih.gov/health/public/sleep/index.htm

National Institute on Neurological Disorders and Stroke: Brain Basics: Understanding Sleep
http://www.ninds.nih.gov/disorders/brain_basics/understanding_sleep.htm

National Sleep Foundation

http://www.sleepfoundation.org

WebMD: Sleep Disorders Health Center

http://www.webmd.com/sleep-disorders-default.htm

ABOUT THE AUTHOR

Mary Brophy Marcus has been a medical writer for over 15 years. She has worked as a writer and editor for *U.S. News & World Report* and *Men's Health* magazines, and is currently a health writer for *USA Today*. She has also contributed to *Self, Shape, National Geographic Traveler, Men's Journal, Georgetown Medicine*, and *The Washington Post*. Brophy Marcus received her Bachelor of Arts from Connecticut College, in New London, Conn., where she double-majored in English and Fine Arts. She also studied cell biology on a PACE Science Journalism fellowship at Harvard Medical School. Brophy Marcus lives outside Washington, DC, in Northern Virginia, with her husband, also a writer, and their two young sons, where they spend many hours in their garden, discovering new insects, planting seeds, and climbing trees.